FOREVER
family

Blessings! *[signature]* Robinson Psalm 139

Laurie Oswald Robinson

Tales of the Times

DEDICATION

For Sarah*
who will always be a part
of our forever family

* Names in this book, except for those of the author,
her husband, and their families, have been changed.

iii |

TABLE OF CONTENTS

SECTION THREE

SECTION FOUR

FOREWORD

I met Laurie Robinson the evening that Kayla Hiebert, a Bethel College social work student, publicly presented her senior thesis describing and analyzing her interviews with foster-to-adopt parents in the child welfare system. I had particularly enjoyed consulting with Kayla about her project because my own dissertation, "Walking a Tightrope: The Role of Resource Parents in Concurrent Planning", also reported on interviews with resource or foster-to-adopt parents in a neighboring state. As I learned that evening, Laurie Robinson was examining the same topic from a very special vantage point; she was writing a first-person account of her own experiences as a foster-to-adopt parent.

Laurie's is an engaging story, hard to put down once begun, complete with reflections and recommendations on the policies and practices that influenced her experience. It is a privilege to hear the honest thoughts and unvarnished feelings about foster care experiences that are seldom shared with such clarity, detail, and openness. In the complex world of child welfare, we struggle to balance preserving families or kin connections with "saving the child". As we ponder what is really in the best interests of the child as well as others involved, it is important to hear the voice of each participant, to see the world from each unique standpoint. Relatively little research has been done to capture the perspective of a resource or foster-to-adopt parent in the child welfare system. Rarer still are detailed narratives told directly by foster-to-adopt parents. Narrative is one of the central ways that individuals order and give meaning to the events of their lives; as professionals and interested members of the public, we garner deeper understanding of the child welfare system if we see through the eyes of each party and learn of the meaning they've assigned to their encounters with the system. Laurie offers an insider's look at the experience of foster-to-adopt parenting and the joys and struggles that emerge. Listening to the voice of such an important player in the foster care drama is an opportunity not to be missed. I am pleased that Kayla introduced me to Laurie Robinson!

Ada Schmidt-Tieszen, LMSW, PhD
Professor of Social Work
Bethel College

PROLOGUE

June 2009

Finally, my cell phone rang.

After I had left for a business meeting an hour away from home, my husband, Al, called. I had been waiting for his call. It would bring news of the next step toward adoption of Sarah. We'd had her in our foster-to-adopt home since she was five and a half months old, and she was nearing thirty months.

The category *foster-to-adopt* meant that we were fostering Sarah with the intent to adopt her for a lifetime if the foster-adoption agency and the courts deemed this to be so. This is different from *foster care*, which describes foster homes not wishing to become a permanent placement. Foster-to-adopt is also different from *respite care*, where foster children occasionally stay in a home for short periods, such as a weekend.

That day prior to Al's call, a *best interest* team of five professionals met to choose between us or Sarah's maternal grandparents as her adoptive *forever family*. During an entire afternoon, the team had reviewed the strengths and needs of Sarah and the two families. They also reported on interactions they'd had with both families and examined the psycho-social histories of both families along with their finances, social worlds, extended families, and education. No stone was left unturned.

"Sweetheart!" Mild-mannered Al shouted into the phone. "They chose us!"

I told my friend standing next to me that I needed to sit down. She steadied me, weakened by the news I had waited so long to receive.

"Really?" Strange as it was, I was not gloriously happy with the outcome. I knew that even though the team had chosen us—and we found out later that they had unanimously agreed that we were the best fit for Sarah—there would be an appeal from the grandparents. We had been told this earlier, and an hour after Al's call we discovered they had appealed this decision.

That now meant that a team of administrators had to review the best interest staffing decision. The administrators would either uphold it or reverse it. They had thirty days to decide.

Because we had engaged an attorney, we also had an appeal opportunity. If the administrators upheld the decision, we would become Sarah's forever family. If the administrators reversed the decision, the maternal grandparents would become her adoptive parents. In the event the administrators reversed the decision, we could appeal that decision in court and would have one last chance to plead our case.

These *ifs* hung heavy in the air and weighed on my heart as Al and I finished our discussion. "What's wrong, sweetheart, you don't sound too happy?" I hesitated. "It's just that I think I've lost my capacity to trust." I said faintly. My friend put her arm around my shoulder.

"I know, Laurie," Al continued, "but we have to hold on. This is one more important step. We're getting there."

"OK," I said, not convinced.

I so wanted to be convinced that the best interest decision was not only one more step, but the last step toward permanency—not only for her but also for us. So many times what I thought was in her best interest had gotten clouded in the storm of other agenda. An uneasiness born from these thoughts kept me from celebrating. I was still on red alert for the next crisis to break out or for the next house of cards to collapse.

As we left the church and drove into the late afternoon sun, ready to set on the prairie, I leaned back in the van seat. "Are you OK?" my friend asked.

"I used to be able to answer a simple question like that," I said as I closed my eyes. "But these days, even the simplest things feel complicated and what appears to be true eventually turns out not to be."

She smiled sadly and patted my hand. I tried to smile back, but it was lame. I just wanted to get back. To Al. To Sarah. To home, where we prayed in the midst of pain, sang in the midst of sadness, forgave in the midst of broken hearts. Home, the thread-bare handhold I had learned to grasp, especially when the powerlessness of being at the mercy of others' decisions threatened to push us over the precipice of grief and loss.

SECTION ONE

Receiving Sarah

Psalm 139: 13–16 (NRSV)
For it was you who formed my inward parts;
you knit me together in my mother's womb.
I praise you, for I am fearfully and wonderfully made.
Wonderful are your works; that I know very well.
My frame was not hidden from you,
when I was being made in secret,
intricately woven in the depths of the earth.
Your eyes beheld my unformed substance.
In your book were written
all the days that were formed for me,
when none of them as yet existed.

CHAPTER ONE

Meeting Sarah

The phone rang in my office in mid-July 2007. The social worker who had trained us to become foster parents was on the other end of the line. "Laurie, we have an emergency. We have a five and a half month old baby girl, Sarah, who needs immediate placement. Will you take her?"

I felt as if someone had punched me in the ribs, and my breath caught. "You mean right now, today?" In my wildest dreams, I hadn't thought it possible our first placement would be a baby. We had earlier completed training to become licensed through the state of Kansas to take children, ages zero to ten, into our home. But babies in the foster-care system were rare, and the youngest we had dared hoped for was an older toddler.

"Yes, right now, today," she said. Even though we had waited for this moment for a year and a half, it seemed too good to be true—and untimely.

"Oh my, we are leaving for a family reunion tomorrow in Beemer, Nebraska, and I don't know. ..."

"You can take her to Nebraska," the social worker charged on. "But you will have to let me know immediately so I can rush down to the court to have a judge sign a release for her to go across state lines. His office closes in a half hour."

I hung up quickly and called my husband, Alfonso (Al) at home.

"Honey, are you sitting down? They have a baby, and they need us to take her immediately, today, right now."

"Hey, slow down, babe," he said, confused. "What do you mean, a baby? And don't forget, they will never let us take her to Nebraska on such short notice."

"No, Al, they will let us. She can go, but we have to decide right now." After silence and a deep breath, he agreed we should take her, and I made the call.

I rushed home to pick up Al, and we headed across town to Wal-Mart. For the first time in our married life—we had married a year and a half earlier in mid-life—we headed to the baby section. We poured over endless choices of cribs and car seats. We chose the mid-range items, and a sales person used a shopping cart to wheel our purchases out of the store and to the trunk of our car.

In five minutes we reached the foster care/adoption agency and walked into the meeting room where social workers swarmed around our tiny daughter-to-be. The first second I laid eyes on her, my heart was swept away, alternately breaking over her plight and flying high with joy.

Her bright smile and charismatic way of drawing everyone in belied all she had been through in the last few days. She was taken from her biological parents because of physical neglect. Police officers had found her in a child seat with a bottle of curdled milk, flies crawling over her unwashed skin. Feces and urine were seeping out from under the bathroom door.

She had been taken to another home. But after a background check, social workers discovered those foster caretakers had unresolved issues in their history, and the professionals decided to move her immediately. She'd been there for a day and a half.

That's when we got the call, and that's when our lives changed forever as we became first-time parents.

Al and I married in September of 2005 when I was forty-six years old and he almost fifty. I had never been married, and he had been married once before, but without children. In fall of 2006, we began the process of searching for a way to become adoptive parents. Al was Panamanian and I was Caucasian, so we were open to adopting mixed-race children like Sarah.

Because we had no means to privately adopt, we went through the Kansas Department of Social Rehabilitation Services (SRS) and an agency it contracted with to provide foster care and adoption services. After many false starts, we connected with an agency that trained us in the spring of 2007 to be eventually licensed through the state of Kansas as a foster-to-adopt home.

The foster-to-adopt category is emotionally brutal. We failed to calculate the emotional costs of agreeing to be foster parents who bonded wholeheartedly and attached with a child, with the possibility she might be reunited with her biological family. But we weren't rich movie stars who could fly to a foreign land to adopt a child. And we didn't have the resources to go through a private adoption agency, free of state involvement.

I bonded with Sarah the first time I laid eyes on her. I'll never forget that late afternoon when the social worker placed the baby girl into my arms. Her deep brown eyes locked with mine as she cuddled in my arms. She fit so comfortably into my embrace that for a moment I almost believed she came from my own body.

As social workers filled out paper work and doted on the baby and us, Al looked at his two women and smiled wide. A man of few words, his joyful grin said it all. He gently guided me and our new child down the hall and out to the car. I held her as Al and the social worker fiddled with the unruly car seat, readying it for our new treasure. We drove home in shock, as I sat in the back seat next to this stranger, who turned into family in the time it took to get a phone call and to make a Wal-Mart run on a hot July afternoon.

CHAPTER TWO

Surviving Shock

July 2007

Cool air-conditioned air hit us in the face as we lugged Sarah and the huge crib box into the house. We dumped it near the door and sat on the couch with our little one. In shock, we passed her back and forth between us; she slept against our chests. We began calling our extended families, our joy uncontainable.

First I called my oldest sister, who lives in Salina, Kansas. "Jane, we have a baby! Can you believe it? I can't believe it." The conversation continued as Al held our tiny bundle. Calls to Al's mother and our brothers, sisters, and friends continued. When Sarah awoke, demanding to be fed, for the first time I prepared formula, rather clumsily. After the calls, Al fumbled with the tangled web of wood and nails that would eventually become her crib.

I sat in the rocking chair I'd gotten after my mom had died, relishing the feel of the tiny, dependent baby against me. Silently, I thanked God for granting us such a human wonder but also breathed a prayer that God would help me be a good mother to this child. Two elements of our parenting would permeate the coming months. Sarah's needs, because of her early trauma, would sometimes be greater and more unpredictable than a well-cared-for infant. And our uncertainty as first-time parents would rear its head as we tried to meet her basic needs as well as help her progress developmentally in areas where she seemed delayed.

With a dreamy grin on my face, I looked at Al. "Honey, what do we do now?" I asked, intoxicated with baby wonder.

"Well, sweetheart, you got me. I guess we just take it one step at a time, beginning with this thing." He peered at the chaotic pile of crib pieces lying at his feet and rubbed his jaw, a gesture he used when stressed.

I pulled up from the rocking chair and took our foster child into our bedroom and laid her, belly down, in the middle of the bed padded with extra blankets. She continued to sleep, still and quiet. I rummaged through the pile of supplies from the social workers—red summer overalls, Onesies©, diapers, bottles, pacifier.

I pulled my eyes from the sleeping child to this pile and wondered, *Is this all she has to her name?* I felt pain as I thought about what brought her to us, and then, back to the task at hand, I wondered, *Do we have enough for the trip to Nebraska tomorrow?* It dawned on me that from now on, preparing to travel would be much more complicated. But I ditched those thoughts as I lay down next to her, watching as her back gently rose and fell with her breathing.

I left her for a time, peeking in now and then to make sure she stayed in the middle of the bed. I was surprised that she seemed unmovable. "Honey, Sarah is so still, do you think something is wrong?" Already the anxious mama, I found myself worrying about her. Near the couch Al lay buried beneath crib-to-be pieces, assorted tools, and a complicated direction sheet.

"These stupid directions." He pushed some of the wood away from him as sweat dotted his T-shirt. Tempted to laugh, I walked away smiling, knowing that he needed space. I found snacks for supper and sat down in the rocking chair to watch.

At about 2 A.M., as I napped on the couch next to Alfonso and his project, he pulled the crib to the doorway of her bedroom adjacent from ours. "Darn!"

His exclamation wakened me. "What's wrong?" I rubbed sleep from my eyes and stared at Al, his expression panicked.

"It is too wide to fit in the doorway!" He jangled and jostled the crib into the doorway a bit tighter. I tried to help, but none of our efforts were successful. There was no choice but to dismantle part of his work and reconstruct it inside the room.

We didn't realize it then, but the crib fiasco foreshadowed the tenor of our unfolding experience with foster parenting. In the days to come, we discovered that every aspect of Sarah's care and our need for increased faith in a God ever-present, as well as solid parenting advice and support, would resemble the complications of putting together this crib. Nothing would be easy. Nearly everything held surprises. And resolving issues surrounding snafus with the system and the biological family would require the utmost commitment and grit.

But at 4 A.M., these larger spiritual and philosophical puzzles were farthest from our minds. All we wanted were a few hours of sleep before we packed our clothes and the bottles and formula for our new baby. Exhausted, we fell into a short sleep, anxious to begin our journey to Nebraska and, even more so, our journey with this child.

CHAPTER THREE
Welcoming Baby

July 2007

I'd heard stories from nieces and nephews about the hassles of traveling with babies and toddlers. But I thought these parents whined too much. The minute my husband drove us out of town and into the prairies, I repented of my judgment. Squeezed in the back seat with Sarah and all her stuff, I shook the baby rattle in her face. She scrunched up with the first eek of a cry. I tried my most cute baby gurgles and *oohs* and *aahs*.

"There, there now." I rustled through a baby bag filled with diapers and formula to find that perfect toy. The toy didn't do much because she was still shut down and dazed, and she fell asleep about an hour later. It may simply have been her attempts to escape my silly child songs and non-stop swishing, rattling and high-pitched sounds.

"Can you believe we are going to Nebraska with a baby?" I asked, ready to doze. For the umpteenth time, I asked my sleep-deprived husband if he wanted me to drive.

"You can drive when we stop for gas," he said groggily. Two hours later, we pulled into a truck stop in York, where we saw the car of my sister and brother-in-law, Vaughn. This was an unplanned rendezvous. They were also going to the family reunion.

They sprang out of their car. "Oh, my!" Jane took the baby from my arms. Sarah smiled and Jane cooed. Sarah stared at my sister as if to say, *Oh, you are the one everyone talks about!*

Jane, the eldest of our family of five siblings had practically raised me, the baby of the family. Our mother had been in poor health as I grew up. Her holding Sarah was like holding a grandchild. With adult children of her own, she had ten grandchildren already, and they adored her. I expected Sarah to follow suit.

It was a huge gift from God that we received Sarah at a time when Jane could be there to give us helpful tips face-to-face. I snatched up every little piece of advice.

Jane's suggestions, coupled with her wonderment about our new situation, infused me with an inner glow. She had waited a long time to see me gratified as a mother. We had tried to get pregnant but to no avail.

Later we pulled into Trail's End, a little hole-in-the-wall hotel where my Dad usually stayed when he came to his boyhood hometown of Beemer for reunions with the Oswald clan. This weekend he suggested we join him there, doubling the reunion with rounds of golf at the nearby course.

We piled out of the car into the hot July blast and struggled to our room with baby in tow. We dumped our bags and changed Sarah's diaper. Jane hovered nearby, just to make sure we were OK. Al and I discussed whether one of us should stay with Sarah in the room while the other went golfing. We decided to take her with us. Sarah would be OK with lots of fluids and a golf cart with a large top for shade.

We looked at each other and laughed. "Wow, did you ever think we would be golfing with a baby?" Al asked as he stroked Sarah's back with tender fatherliness.

"No, but maybe she will help our golf score," I quipped, as I stuffed the diaper bag with supplies and added ice to her water. We piled into the car and headed out to the golf course, where for the next two and a half hours, we held this precious gift in our sweaty arms. We handed her over to each other and let her ride with Jane and Vaughn some as we hit our balls and scored our card.

She didn't help our score, but she cured me for good of taking the game of golf— or any other pursuit—quite as seriously as before. The weightiness of being responsible for a dependent suddenly far outstripped any other goal. We weren't the first parents to discover that a child changes everything in your life—how you do what you do, when you do it, how often you do it. And for us weekend golfers, in love with the game, putting a little round ball into a little round cup didn't seem quite as crucial as it once had.

What did seem crucial, however, was how still and silently Sarah slept. We became concerned the trauma of her crisis had induced an emotional and physical shut-down. "What should we do?" I asked Al and Jane.

"Right now I think she is pretty shut down. Eventually she should come out of her shock." Jane's knowledge comforted us again. For almost fifteen years, she had worked in early childhood education as a program director and was deeply aware of what trauma can do to a child and how it can affect development. Fortunately for us, she believed good nurturing and positive parenting could help heal some of the early trauma. She also knew we were ready to give Sarah our full attention, our entire life.

In the hours ahead, we learned how to manage diaper changes, sleep schedules, and formula preparation.

Other than the basics, we knew very little about Sarah. The first hours with a foster child can be deceptive. Up to this point, Sarah had been shut down, so all seemed smooth. That would not last.

The first night, Al and I cobbled together the traveling baby crib,—it was easier to put together than her crib at home—and fixed a little nest in the center of it. Like the days ahead, we fought over who would get to feed Sarah. The excitement of having a little body hunkering down into you never quite wore off.

Al won out, and he got to give her the last feeding of the day. The sight of bare-chested daddy holding a tiny baby, wearing only a diaper, was never as sweet as that first night. There would be many times he would hold Sarah like that, cuddling his little girl, dreaming of the future when she would say her first words, take her first step, read her first book, play her first soccer game, perform her first piano recital, kiss her first boy.

But the question deep in our hearts was: Would we keep her long enough to watch her life unfold? As foster-to-adopt parents, we opened ourselves to that possibility. But unbeknownst to us, we also left ourselves wide open for the biggest roller coaster ride we would ever take emotionally and spiritually, a journey that would dizzy and disorient us.

That night, what we didn't know didn't hurt us. Blissfully, we spooned and looked over our backs at our baby, sleeping soundly in her soft blankets, her little back moving up and down. Several times that night, one or both of us got up to see if she was still OK. It was only the first thirty-six hours, and we were an anxious and happy wreck.

CHAPTER FOUR

Remembering Childhood

July 2007

Al and I wheeled Sarah in her stroller into the VFW Hall, the site of the Oswald reunion. My brother Neil, and his wife, Kathy, and cousins clustered round us. My dad, in his upper eighties, beamed as we took Sarah out of her stroller to a waiting circle of hugs and kisses. The Oswald clan was expressive and artistic—never short on tears, laughter, stories, or touch.

As I watched this play out with our foster daughter, images of former reunions emerged. I remembered Dad's sisters—my aunts Helen, Ruth, and Esther—hugging me until I got lost in their heavily-bosomed embraces, wondering if I would ever come out again! For years, I had wanted to attend a family reunion with my own family—not just as the baby of Paul and Dorothy's family of five children. This time, I had a husband and a baby of my own. It was special for me to introduce my husband and our formerly neglected child to this warm and loving extended family.

"Hey, little one, come to your uncle," cooed brother Neil, a baby lover. He jiggled and hugged her until Kathy took her for a few minutes. People lined up for the noon meal as Al and I took turns feeding Sarah her bottle and then eating our own meal of chicken and the fixings as well as pie and coffee. We fed and burped her as coffee smells wafted across the long tables.

As we juggled bottles and diaper changes, more family came over to engage with her. Slowly she seemed to be melting from the earlier shock as she grinned and wiggled her little body, all decked out in her newest outfit of overalls and baby running shoes. Judging from her responses, we believed she hadn't received this kind of attention and touch, and she seemed to absorb the love with glee. My dad, at various points, said, "Look at my youngest granddaughter, isn't she something?"

I remembered something about my own parents I had forgotten. It wasn't unusual in my childhood home in Manson, Iowa, where my dad owned a John Deere implement business, for Mom to set an extra place at our table. There in the extra place sat pastors, in hot water over something or other in our congregation, fed from Mom's basic but great-tasting food and from my parents' acceptance and compassion. Also in that place sat Nassum, our family's foreign exchange student from Afghanistan in the 1966–67 school year. He said morning and evening prayers by facing east toward Mecca, and our nearest city, Fort Dodge, sixteen miles east on Highway 7. I remembered peeking through the keyhole of his bedroom door. He sat hunched over, mumbling his Islamic prayers.

There were a couple of years when Jane, who had worked as a nurse at the women's reformatory in Rockwell City, Iowa, brought home inmates for a weekend leave. These friendly, but rough-around-the-edges, women also sat at our table, inhaling Mom's spaghetti and meatballs, tacos, chili, and brownies. I stared at them from my perch next to brother Brian and thought, *These women seem just like us. They like family, they like Mom's food, they laugh, they talk. I wonder why they have to be in jail?*

I had no way of knowing then how hospitable my parents were compared to many folks in our small, farming community in the center of the richest and blackest soil in the world. I just thought that was how all families were. Their modeling indeed planted the seed of hospitality in my heart and had helped form my adult decision to become a foster-to-adopt parent.

In the midst of these family strengths, I also remembered our weaknesses. We had our share of trouble, too, in my immediate and extended family. My dad's youngest brother had committed suicide in Vietnam. Jane's first husband had abandoned her and their two-year-old daughter. Stories abounded of alcoholism and depression. One relative wound up in a state institution for mental illness. My own mother, a wonderful and generous woman, had also not been well when I was growing up. She suffered a variety of depressions, major surgeries, and bouts of cancer and heart problems. She passed away from heart failure in 1995, when I was thirty-five. Though we had a stormy relationship for many years, in part from a lack of early bonding and attachment, we made our peace the week before she died.

All this wafted through my mind during this reunion, especially after lunch when we watched a video, created by Cousin Rolland from Seattle, about three generations of the Oswalds. Included was information about how my great-grandfather Jacob Oswald was born out of wedlock in Germany and became an orphan when his mother died. As I gazed over at our sleeping child, I mused how the prerequisite for loving and wanting a child is not always based on biological ties. In fact, we wouldn't even be the same extended family today if it weren't for the family who took in my great-grandfather and raised him to become the healthy young man who married my great-grandmother Margaretha. They raised my twelve great aunts and uncles, including Grandpa Jacob, the oldest of that family, who married Elizabeth, my grandmother. She gave birth to eight children, including my father.

As big-meal sleepiness seeped over all of us, the video ended and so did my musings. It was time to take Sarah back to the hotel. We later returned for the evening talent program and then went back to the hotel room to settle down for the night, in much the same way as the night before. Al discovered that Sarah's little body could drape nicely over his tummy, and there she lay as he watched sports on TV and I read until it was time to put her in the traveling crib for the night. As I fed her, I looked into her deep brown eyes. She was drowsy and contented. I stroked her cheeks and bald head. I leaned down to smell her skin—full of innocence, baby lotion, and vulnerability.

Two generations ago, Great-Grandpa was taken in like this by a family. They wanted him and kept him, and he belonged. Would this child's fate be the same? As I put her in the crib, my husband's snores filled the room, and my thoughts swirled with the happy delirium of feeling needed by someone so little and so dependent. I spooned around my husband's back and lay sleepless. My mind filled with gratefulness for the way my clan had accepted this unknown child and turned her into family. Stranger things have happened but nothing more beautiful.

CHAPTER FIVE

Traveling Blind

July 2007

As we left the reunion, we stopped for gas, soda, and wet wipes at the gas station on Beemer's outskirts and headed home. What faced us there was a foreign land of baby bottles, lukewarm baths, and bedtime books. Sarah and I sat listless in the back seat, wilted from the heat. Al drove southwest into the late afternoon Nebraska sun as Sarah napped. I stared at the damage a baby's things can do to a backseat. Rattles, cloth books, formula cans, and Alco sacks with baby clothes were stuffed in crevices and under front seats. I swigged Diet Pepsi and stared out the window, too tired to order the mess.

"Honey, what have we done?" I asked.

"I don't know, sweetheart, but it's going to change our lives." He changed the radio to oldies. As tunes drifted through the car, I thought about how the family reunion demonstrated that Sarah, no matter what her bloodline, was accepted by my family.

Still amazed, I quizzed Al. "So, honey, did your family ever have reunions like this?"

"No, not like this. Leave it up to the Oswalds. But my brothers and I have managed to help Mom celebrate her birthdays, and we get together at weddings and other big events." Al was fathered in Panama by a man who abandoned Al and his mother. She then married an African-American soldier, with whom she had four sons—Al's half brothers.

Al's family had traveled around the globe, living in Germany, Panama, Colorado, and Kansas. Because of trouble in the home, Al had a broken childhood. I knew this pain is what infused his love of Sarah with caring gentleness and quiet passion. He was a dedicated uncle to his brothers' kids. He also had worked for fifteen years at the YMCA in Salina where he coached kids' teams and worked with teenagers.

In his first marriage a decade and a half ago, he and his former wife fostered several older children, but never a baby. They enjoyed being foster parents until an incident occurred. Al told me how a social worker demanded a twelve-year-old boy in their care be allowed to hang a picture in his room of a scantily clad woman. That was when they stopped fostering. They wanted to provide more guidance and have a say-so in what they saw as questionable behavior. But the social workers had demanded the boy had his rights.

That experience soured Al. So the day I told him that we had gotten a call back from a social worker who would help us train to become foster parents, he was uncertain. I was happy that after six months of calling to various agencies, we had finally made a connection, but he was sobered. He capitulated to my wishes even though he felt the system was broken and needed reform. But we were still early in our marriage, and he loved children and wanted to please me.

The sounds of Sarah rousing from her nap shook me from my daydreaming. Her wails filled our small Ford Escort. She didn't want toys; she didn't want her bottle. What did she want? After a dry diaper in York and a change of scenery, she settled again, Mommy at her side cooing, singing, and stroking her soft head.

As the first stars appeared in the navy-turquoise of evening dusk, I panicked. Here we were just ordinary people, hoping to provide wholeness, care, and nurture to this broken child. Could we pull it off? I thought about all the tasks I needed to do the next day to baby-size our home and to make a nest that would hold this hungry, needy little one close to our hearts. Like any new parent, I doubted my abilities, though I never doubted we wanted her with us. We would give her everything we had.

"God, help us," I prayed as sleep drifted down on the backseat. It carried our motley little family, thrown together by God's mysterious ways, into an unknown future.

CHAPTER SIX

Settling In

Early August 2007

Sarah, Al, and I began to settle into each other's lives, and in our bumbling, giddy way, we managed a schedule. Al worked three to eleven. He'd sleep in the mornings as I took Sarah out for a 10:00 A.M. stroll. Since it was now the hottest part of summer, I'd walk down the block with the most shade and slurp my coffee as I cooed, "Look at that birdie! Oh, there's a doggie!" I'd sing nursery rhymes and bend down to look into her eyes and smile. I'd check to make sure she had enough juice and that her bonnet was shading her face. But it took me awhile to realize this little person was not going to answer. That didn't keep me from chirping a description about everything I saw. Lots of times, she fell asleep. That should have told me something about how boring my adult drone was. But neither one of us was worse for wear of that morning ritual.

Our elderly next-door neighbor got a kick out of watching me walk down our cul-de-sac with this baby in the umbrella stroller. Colleen loved to stop us on our route and tease me, "So what are you two doing this morning?" She'd bend down and lightly stroke Sarah's head and coo. During the next several months not one day went by when Colleen didn't come over just to hold Sarah on our front stoop as I rushed to complete small chores. This woman, known as a rascally soul about town, became a pussycat in Sarah's presence.

We felt the euphoria of sharing Sarah with our doting and loving extended families. But we also felt the weight of being on call 24-7. No longer could we golf or run to our favorite restaurant at the drop of a hat. Watching a movie after supper was out because we fell asleep after the first ten minutes. Formula-making, Sarah jiggling and schedule-regulating zapped us. Making sure she was dry, happy, and stimulated took all our energies. We also had no clue about her former schedule and just had to guess.

Fortunately, my sister Jane loves babies. Besides being a mother and grandmother, she knows not only the latest research about what babies need to develop healthily, but also the telltale signs they are lagging in certain areas. When I called to tell her that Sarah wanted to eat all the time or had gotten yet another cold that wouldn't go away, Jane calmed me. She also had connections to professionals who could counsel me. I spent an afternoon with her former coworkers, who talked with me about my concerns regarding Sarah.

We soon learned that the art of foster parenting included balancing the sense of normal child development with identifying what behaviors may come from Sarah's early neglect. From the start, we felt Sarah had not been talked to, sung to, or stimulated much. I bought kids' books, CDs, and tapes and became intimately acquainted with the baby aisles in local stores.

Many of our greatest baby finds came from friends in a Sunday school class. Because their own kids were grown, they wanted to rid their garages of unused baby stuff. I was thankful for their gifts and even more thankful for their understanding. They had been where I was now. It felt strange to be mothering a baby when many friends were empty nesters.

In the first season of our caring for Sarah, she and I were alone for long evenings because of Al's evening shift work. Several times girlfriends brought supper and sat with us to eat and to chat in our living room. Sometimes we went for walks in the Kansas dusk. They watched as I bathed Sarah, lathered her with lotion, and sat in the chair to read *Where Do Kisses Come From?* While my friends stayed, I rocked her to sleep. They had been used to seeing me single and then married without children.

I had entered this strange land for which I did not have road maps. Instead of a highway of well-marked directions, a wild, rushing river of love carried me along. Al and I had fallen in love with this little girl who was not our own but each day would become so more and more. This river would take us over some falls in the days ahead.

CHAPTER SEVEN

Letting Go?

Late August 2007

During our fifth week with Sarah, an agency social worker stopped by. "Laurie and Al, we have done a home study on a paternal grandfather who has checked out OK, and Sarah will go to live with him next week."

I felt as if my breath had gotten knocked out of me, and I heard little of what she said next. I leaned hard against Al and grasped his hand. I waited to cry until she left. Our hearts had been swept away by this tiny girl with dark eyes and great grin. Her winsome spirit drew us into her circle, and it would not be easy to untangle from this web of growing attachment. Al held me and reached for a Kleenex. "It will be OK, sweetheart," he said. We held each other as our minds and hearts twisted with daydreams of what might have been if she could have stayed with us.

During the next week, we bought new clothes to send with her along with tote bags, diapers, other goodies, and a small picture album. Our families wanted to see her before she left, so we went visiting.

On the evening before she was to leave and without Al along to help, I took her to the home of my niece Shan where our extended family was having a birthday party. Jane and Vaughn and nieces and nephews gathered to celebrate birthdays and to say good-bye to Sarah. The youngest of our clan, Addie, had grown close to Sarah. It was fun for Addie to have someone younger than herself in the family, and she loved playing the big sister.

After the party, it was time to change and feed Sarah, and the kids all helped. They took turns holding and feeding her. One of the oldest, Jackson, changed her diapers. Addie stayed close to Sarah and stroked her hair and kissed her cheeks.

Jane and I had a few quiet minutes before we left, as I pulled her aside. "Jane, why did Al and I do this? It is just so hard."

She stroked my back and reached for Kleenexes for us both. "I know, Laurie, but you have to realize how much love you've brought her in such a short time."

"I know, but when she leaves tomorrow, I will have a hole in my heart the shape of Sarah, and no one will ever be able to fill it."

"We all will have holes in our heart the shape of Sarah," she said in a wavering voice as she helped me pack baby stuff in the car. We walked back to the house to have the kids say good-bye.

No one wanted to let her go, and the entire tribe moved along with me as I carried her. One kid held her hand, another kid held my hand, another kid stroked her hair.

"Bye, Sarah, bye-bye," they shouted and waved as I drove into the Kansas night to connect with I-135 for one of the longest rides of my life. In the rearview mirror, blurred by my emotions, I saw a family grieving someone who so quickly had become a part of us. The collective hole in our hearts was so deep as to be incalculable.

† † †

The next morning as we were packing up Sarah's things, the phone rang.

"Can you come down to our office right now?" our social worker asked.

Shocked, I stuttered, "But … but … I thought you were going to come and get her this afternoon?"

"There's been a new development, and we need you to come to the office."

I got off the phone and repeated to Al what she said. "What is going on?"

His gentle eyes, normally so placid, stirred with emotion. "I don't know but anything can happen at this point," he said.

We buckled Sarah into the car seat as Al drove out of the driveway. My heart skipped beats as I tried to absorb what this mystery meeting might yield. We got to the agency and carted in Sarah and all her stuff.

"The social worker guided us into the small room that afforded some privacy.

Sarah's paternal grandfather sat on the couch. He was wringing his hands and nervously smiling as the social worker introduced us.

"I just can't do this. … I can't take Sarah," he said as he looked down to the floor.

Al and I exchanged glances as he explained further. His son, Sarah's father, had anger-management issues, and he was making life rough for those around him. We had already experienced this reality during the first several times we'd dropped Sarah off at the agency for visits with her birth parents. It seemed to us that Sarah's mother was a gentle and caring soul but also passive in the wake of the more aggressive stance of the father. He tended to push his anxieties and frustrations outward.

"It is just too much to take on right now, because our family situation is so complicated," the grandfather said. "I don't think it would be good for Sarah."

My breath came out in short tufts as I tried to focus in the midst of my blurring vision. I looked over at Al, who was trying to entertain Sarah.

"So, what does this mean?" I directed my question to the social worker.

"It means you can take her home again—if you want her."

If we want her? My heart soared as I reached over and grabbed Sarah and held her close to my chest, near to the hole being filled up again with this baby who would still be part of our family—at least for now.

CHAPTER EIGHT

Breaking Trust

Early September 2007

About three weeks later, I went to pick up Sarah at the agency after her weekly visit with her biological parents. Her father, a thin, agitated man, rushed over to me. Social workers had warned me he was skittish about the number of colds Sarah had and was asking a lot of questions about whether we were caring for her properly.

My insides tightened as I reached to take Sarah from his arms and faced his interrogation. The agency had recently decided foster-to-adopt parents should be considered as resources to parents who lost custody of their children and were working to get them back. So we were given the new name "resource parents." I felt like anything but a resource. Her father seemed to disdain me and everything I stood for.

"Haven't you been taking Sarah to the doctor?" His gaze burned into mine. "I am really worried about her."

"Yes, we have been taking her to the doctor, but we need to schedule another visit since the latest cold," I said stiffly, feeling trapped. I told the social worker I'd call her later.

As soon as we got home, I vented my anger to Al about being bullied. Then I called to make a doctor's appointment for Sarah. The experience at the office made me uneasy about even waiting a day.

"I am calling to make an appointment with the doctor about Sarah's latest cold," I said to the nurse on the other end of the line.

"I am really confused," the nurse said. "Her father just called and made an appointment for her."

"What?" I was stunned. "I'll be right there." I felt Sarah's father didn't trust me to care for his daughter. I felt betrayed, confused, and ashamed. He accused us of negligence although nothing was further from the truth. I hated being given the responsibility of caring for her and yet not being trusted to do the job.

I packed Sarah into the car and drove across town to the medical clinic. Her social worker, Jackie, was there waiting for us.

"What in God's name is going on here?" I asked.

"I know, I know. This is crazy," she said, attempting to calm me. "He shouldn't have done that, but he did and now we're here."

"And you people wonder why you can't get enough foster families," I ranted. "This kind of crap happens and they leave. I don't blame them!"

"Laurie, I will go into the doctor's office with you because Sarah's dad also made claims that you and Al have been physically abusing her. He says he's seen scratches and bruises on her legs. I have to go in with you to witness the doctor confirming this is not true. I am so sorry, Laurie. We know it's not true, but we are required to follow up."

I pushed and pulled at the wet Kleenex, shedding pill-sized pieces of white tissue onto the carpet. I felt sick and dizzy and as pulverized as the tissue. The nurse called us in, and the doctor, clearly agitated by the confusion, was terse and inhospitable. He undressed Sarah and checked for abuse. Finding none, he discussed remedies for her cold. When he saw how upset I was, he softened some, but it was too late.

Sarah had no bruises, but my trust in the foster care system was bruised even though the social workers were following protocol and were not indicting us personally. Rational or not, I felt that even if the doctor wrote a report absolving us of abuse, no one could heal the shame we had endured. As foster parents, we were asked to swim in a fish bowl of scrutiny, bombarded by expectations of the agency and mistrust of the biological family. If anyone needed a doctor that day, it was me. If only my malady was as simple as a cold. A virus of anger and sadness had entered my heart that no earthly medicine could cure.

SECTION TWO

Raising Sarah

Psalm 139: 1–6 (NRSV)
O Lord, You have searched me and known me.
You know when I sit down and when I rise up;
you discern my thoughts from far away.
You search out my path and my lying down,
and are acquainted with all my ways.
Even before a word is on my tongue, O Lord,
you know it completely.
You hem me in, behind and before,
and lay your hand upon me.
Such knowledge is too wonderful for me;
it is so high I cannot attain it.

CHAPTER NINE

Sacrificing Plans

Late September 2007

Early morning light fell across my Bible and cup of coffee as I sat in the recliner, absorbing the quiet before Sarah awakened. It was late September and the month of reckoning. For the past several weeks, I had juggled mothering with my part-time job as the editor of a Mennonite women's magazine. I had also entered a biblical studies program at a local college. I had been accepted into the program a couple of months before Sarah arrived. My long-range plan had been to finish seminary so I could follow what had seemed to be a call to pastoral work.

But this morning I had a sense that my schedule was not sustainable and that I needed to pull back. I was a driven person and not accustomed to quitting. I was loyal to my commitments and thorough. Those qualities had brought me this far, and I hated to drop anything. But the realities of nurturing a little person while dodging the land mines of the foster care system were washing upon me. All of this was no small feat for a forty-nine year old foster mom.

As I read Isaiah 43:18-19 (NRSV) for morning devotions, I realized God was speaking to me and that it was time to heed that still small voice. It was clamoring for some attention within the roar of the tsunami of my responsibilities. "Do not remember the former things, or consider the things of old. I am about to do a new thing; now it springs forth, do you not perceive it? I will make a way in the wilderness and rivers in the desert."

I knew that it was time to make way for new things, time to quit my part-time job and school. I saw no other way around the fact that my energies were limited. I needed and wanted to prioritize caring for Sarah. But I still had to work to help bring in income. I could now begin the freelance business I had dreamed of for a long time. Until my options narrowed, I didn't have the guts to do it. But my back was against the wall. I had to cut an opening to let in some air before I suffocated. I needed to make way for this new season in my life, this new little person in my care.

I waited until Sarah was down for her morning nap before I broke the news to Al.

"Honey, I have to do this." I watched as a gathering storm of conflict and confusion darkened his face.

"But sweetheart, are you sure this is what you want to do? You have made so many changes in our short time together. You quit a full-time job when we got married. And then you took a new part-time job and applied for school. Then we got Sarah. And now you want to quit school after six weeks of classes?"

His questions felt more like an indictment rather than a quest for answers. I turned away and banged dishes around the kitchen. Life since Sarah brought new marital issues, and this was one for the books.

My hands became red from twisting the dish towel so hard. "You don't want me to change so you will feel more comfortable, is that it? Just because you don't like change doesn't mean I shouldn't change when to do so would be better for all of us."

The frying pan I threw into the sink clanged so hard I thought Sarah would wake up. Thankfully, she slept through the mayhem, and we calmed down enough to stay in the same room and talk more.

"OK, sweetheart, I'll back you," Al conceded. He seemed to want to make peace more than to agree with my decision, which angered me even more. He got up and went downstairs to watch TV. I busied myself with housework.

Later in the day, I called the school and set up an appointment to cancel my classes. I also called my work supervisor regarding my editorship. Within the week, I was no longer in school and had agreed to stay with the magazine for six months until a new editor could be found. I had been a writer and editor for much of my adult life, but I had never been a mother. There would be other chances to write, but this could be my last chance to be a mother.

That evening during Sarah's bath, I poured water in and out of pails and pushed her rubber ducky beneath the water. I gave her belly a peck with the duck's orange beak. She giggled as I tickled her and prepared the washcloth and baby shampoo to wash her head, still bald but softening with slow-growing baby hair.

As I lathered her head, I thought back to earlier in the day when I had argued with my husband. The feelings of joy in playing with our baby and feelings of pain evoked by our changes were all part of parenting. I wondered, *Do other parents feel this way, too?*

Some of the best times Sarah and I spent together were after her bath when I wrapped her dripping body in a big purple towel and carried her to our bed. I plopped her down and dried her quickly as she squiggled out of the towel and romped on the down comforter.

For fifteen minutes like this every evening, we played games—patty cake, peekaboo, and this little piggy. I acted as if I couldn't catch her as she crawled to the other side of the bed. Then I sang "The Itsy Bitsy Spider," "Old McDonald," and "Rock-a-Bye Baby" in hopes of calming her down. Though only semi-successful, I scooped her up and took her to the changing table. I rubbed her with lotion, dusted her with powder, and put on her diaper and sleeper, singing to her all the while.

My sister's advice on child development told me that games, songs, and healthy touch help a baby's brain develop and make critical cognitive connections. Jane told me about studies conducted in the 1960s by David Hubel and Torsten Wiesel. They found that vision does not develop normally in cats if the eye and brain fail to make connections during a critical window of time in early life. In the test, one eye of each kitten was held closed after birth. After several weeks the restraint was removed, and none of the kittens could see out of the eye that had been closed even though it was perfectly normal.

Research showed that if some stages of development aren't made at critical times, they can't be made. I was going to do all I could to help Sarah's brain cells grow and connect.

"OK, punkin pie," I cooed as I took her into my arms and carried her out to the fridge to get her night bottle. Sarah grabbed for it as I plunked down in the recliner and opened *Where's Spot*. She sucked on her bottle, and I began to read. It was one of the few books that engaged her the whole way through, and so it was my favorite story, too. Her eyes got heavy as the milk slowed and her sucking continued. I rose from the chair and carried her to her room. The transition to the crib was a delicate one and required great finesse. If I didn't want a battle cry from her, I needed to do this just right.

I whispered a prayer, one that I had whispered from Day One. "Dear Lord, let Sarah know how much we love her and you love her and help her to grow up to be the person you created her to be."

I clicked the door shut and fell exhausted into bed, relieved my day of decision to quit school and job was done. As I fell asleep, I thought about the sacrifices I was about to make for this child. She wasn't mine but had become one of the greatest joys of living. Siblings and friends had conveyed to me that there is nothing quite as satisfying as parenting. I hadn't believed them. Until one reads *Where's Spot?* for the hundredth time, to a baby nestling in your arms and smelling of lotion, one doesn't know this.

But now I knew.

No degree or paycheck could ever feel as rich as the knowledge that this evening after her bath I helped a child make new connections with herself, her caretakers, and her world. Since I had decided not to stay in school, I wouldn't be privy to the knowledge of seminary teachers. But on this night and so many nights to come, I was Sarah's teacher, a job no one else could fill during these critical months.

CHAPTER TEN

Enjoying Firsts

Christmas 2007, Winter 2008

My eighty-nine year old dad sat in the recliner and opened his Christmas gifts. Al and I sat on the floor with Sarah and helped her rip hers open. We wanted her to get to the gifts so she could play, but she liked the shredded paper better. Soon she climbed into her new red wagon with her new stuffed animals and new book, *Goodnight Moon*. Al snapped photos of me reading to her as we sat in a mountain of wrappings. Dad put on another pot of coffee, and Al put together her new push toy.

I smiled at the happy chaos around me. Did it get much better than this? A baby's first Christmas. An elderly father who was still active. A husband who loved me and loved our foster daughter. Christmas carols playing in the background. A new wagon and other gifts of love. And Sarah, our little one, ready to take her first steps and say her first words.

Sarah's squeals broke into my reflections as she pulled on my arms to get out of the wagon. She fingered her push toy and gummed its pink, turquoise, and yellow parts. I watched for new signs of her wanting to walk and to actually push the thing. Not today, I admitted. Instead, she crawled across the room in flash time to investigate our two cats. She grabbed Kit Kat's grey-black and white fur, sending the traumitized cat to the basement. Tabby was a little more patient but soon followed his brother.

Anyone who has watched a baby grow knows the joys of her firsts. For a foster child, firsts can be delayed by earlier trauma. Her firsts were also complicated by weekly interruptions such as visits with biological parents, social workers, and other professionals. To stay on top of how Sarah was developing in the midst of this crazy-quilted life, we asked early childhood professionals to evaluate her. After testing her twice, a professional said Sarah was progressing well with gross- and fine-motor and verbal skills. Deluged with books, music, talking, and touching, Sarah was thawing out from earlier shutdown and was laughing, playing, and voicing consonants.

During the Christmas holidays Al and I noticed a leap forward in her language and mobility. She was bored with the safe living room floor and her usual toys. She cruised to the lower cupboards to pull things out and pulled herself up to the coffee tables. We also noticed an increase in attachment and bonding. She wanted to be near us all the time and looked directly into our eyes. We blew her kisses and she'd laugh as she clumsily tried to blow them back. And we used sign language for "please" and "more" at meals.

When we took her shopping, her winning smile and charisma drew people close. It didn't take long before she'd wrap folks around her little finger. We noticed how hyper-vigilant she was everywhere. She seemed cautious of new people and new surroundings, which signaled her growing attachment to us. But it also marked her need to be in control, a likely response to early trauma.

Her rapid progress continued into February when it was time to throw a first birthday bash. More than twenty friends and family members rang our doorbell for the evening pizza and ice cream party.

"Sarah!" shouted the kids from our families. They dropped their coats and mittens in a heap and ran to Sarah, special to all of them. They kissed and hugged her and drug her along with them into her room where they played on the floor.

Later Sarah sat in her high chair wide-eyed as the huge ONE on her cake flickered and we sang "Happy Birthday." We put on her bib and set the cake in front of her. Soon, chocolate was everywhere as all of us laughed together and marveled at this blossoming child.

After cake and ice cream we crammed into the living room, where all the kids sat with Sarah. They helped her open her tower of gifts—stuffed animals, two *Winnie the Pooh* board books with flaps, and other toys with bells, lights, and whistles. After the gift-opening mayhem, everyone formed a circle to pray for Sarah. But first, I thanked everyone.

"Al and I thank you for being a part of our lives and a part of Sarah's life," I said as Al handed me Kleenex. "We don't know how long she will be with us, but you have all been part of giving her a great start."

Prayers came easily from several people around the circle, including my sister. "Please let Sarah know how much you love her, and let Al and Laurie know how much you love them," she prayed through her tears. "Keep them all safe in your arms and help them deal with all that is still to come their way."

As I cleaned up and threw away paper plates smeared with chocolate, I realized the party marked the end of Sarah's first tumultuous year. But it also signaled a new year, full of unknowns. Would the system decide to send her back home? Or would the courts terminate parental rights? Would grandparents or other kin emerge as caretakers, or would we be able to adopt her?

Especially on her birthday, those questions plagued me, as the clock ticked toward an uncertain future. Our hearts beat ever more deeply with love for her, our lives attached ever more strongly to hers. Something deep inside me whispered, *Guard your heart*. But another whisper, deeper still, replied, *It is already captured*.

CHAPTER ELEVEN

Melting Down

March 2008

The new family social worker for Sarah's parents took me aside after I dropped Sarah off for one of her twice-weekly visits with them at the foster care office.

"Laurie, we've made a decision. From now on, Sarah will be visiting her parents in their new apartment. It's time to see if they are ready for home visits away from this office. Don't worry. I will drop in unannounced a couple times each visit to make sure everything is OK."

I thought, *Don't worry?* The news flipped on my mama-bear switch. A rush of fear and protectiveness flashed through me. "Are you sure about this?" Sarah's father had trouble with anger management. And her parents had been kicked out of other living situations because of filth and inability to pay their bills. I also worried Sarah's increased mobility and determination could set off his anger, and then what? This could be a train wreck.

"If anything happens to Sarah—anything—I am coming after you!" As soon as the words flew out of my mouth, I knew they were wrong, but there was no pulling them back. The social worker, a short, timid young woman, drew back from me but tried to mask her shock at my brazen behavior.

"It will be OK," she nearly whispered. "This is what we are required to do—give the family as many opportunities to grow as possible. We'll keep you informed."

"I'm sorry about what I just said, I didn't mean it, but … but … but I just want our baby to be safe," I stammered as I left the office. My hands shook. I started the car and headed home.

My mind raced into a thousand scenes. I was afraid Sarah could get hurt, and I was mad about losing control. This was not the first time, nor would it be the last that it felt like our home was a hotel. It seemed we shouldered all the responsibilities for Sarah's daily care but none of the privileges of making important decisions on her behalf.

A couple hours after I got home, our phone rang.

"Laurie, this is Jackie, your social worker. Do you have some time to talk?"

"Ah, yeah," I said, dreading the conversation.

"The family support worker filed a report about how you threatened her. Is that true?"

I was mute, paralyzed. She continued in my silence.

"If it is true, you simply cannot talk this way to our staff."

"But you don't understand. You ask me to care for Sarah, and then you don't want me to care about where she goes and what she does. I don't get it. So what now? Are we fired?"

"Calm down, Laurie. We aren't taking Sarah away from you. You are doing a wonderful job. But you must be careful how you express yourself to social workers."

"But you still don't understand. I am trying to take care of Sarah the best I know how, but you won't let me!" Residue of my childhood arose with a vengeance. As a child, I also had endured some trauma. It included suffering the absence of Mother when her many sicknesses took her out of our home for extended hospital stays. And I had been unaware until now of what I vowed: I would save any child in my care from undue pain at all costs. Sarah's visit with her parents in their new apartment felt unsafe to me. In allowing this, I felt as if I were breaking my pact to protect our little girl.

My reaction to the social worker had more to do with my past than it did with immediate danger to Sarah. Jackie's gentle prodding about what was going on helped me realize I needed more healing regarding my childhood.

Foster families, including us, come into the system with good intentions. But all the best intentions in the world don't undo the fact that many of the decisions about Sarah's life would be made by professionals and not by us.

Later that evening, in trying to settle Sarah down for the night, I realized my stormy state had set off anxiety in her. After her bath and bottle, she continued to wail and fuss. I stood up from the recliner to rock her in my arms. When that didn't work, I put on a CD of James Taylor and stood close to the amplifier. "Good night you moonlight ladies, rockabye Sweet Baby James. Deep greens and blues are the colors I choose so let me go down in my dreams. Oh rock-a-bye Sweet Baby James."

Ever so slowly, her little body let go into the sounds of the sweet ballad. She was teaching me that fretting about the past or worrying about the future would not bring rest. This moment, as uncertain as it was, was all we had. At the end of the day, all of us, no matter how old we are, need the comfort of knowing strong arms will hold us when we cry. They'll keep us safe from the bumps in the night we cannot control.

CHAPTER TWELVE
Facing Consequences

March 2008

Ashamed of my behavior and reprimanded roundly, I settled into an uneasy routine with the new arrangement. Twice each week, either Al or I took Sarah to her parent's apartment across town. We traversed the broken-down front stoop to the door. The first time we went to the door, three puppies tangled around our feet. Two more were yipping in the living room, a sight that delighted Sarah.

As soon as she saw their little black bodies wiggling around her, she was off and running, ready to play. But increasingly there were signs that just as puppies become bigger dogs, so can seemingly harmless visits turn into bigger issues.

One day after picking her up, Al came home fired up. "There were cigarette butts overflowing on the TV." He paced the floor. "I think I should call the social worker."

"Ha, good luck with that," I growled, still sore about my run-in with the agency staff. As I popped open a Diet Coke, I studied my husband's face, searching for other signs of alarm. "What else did you see?"

More unwilling than me to be hard on others, he replied, "Well, those dogs. I don't think the parents pick up after them, if you know what I mean." His eyes glistened. "She was playing by herself as her daddy slept and her mommy watched TV."

He took a jug of milk from the fridge and rifled through a bag of cookies. Eating couldn't cure our plight, but it was one thing we could control. It pained Al when he saw Sarah in that situation. Al's time with Sarah was spent playing, romping, and caring for her; in quiet moments she snuggled and fell asleep in his arms or on his tummy.

"Al, just call someone," I said, piqued by my fear and lack of control. He left a voice message for the social worker. She called back later.

"She said she didn't see cigarette butts." He cradled his head in his hands.

"Didn't see them, or didn't want to see them?" I had no mercy for the system at this point. I had been told federal and state mandates required agencies to give birth parents multiple chances to clean up their lives in order to get their kids back. But whose job was it to protect the child?

A few weeks after the incident between the staff person and me, I asked our social worker and her supervisor to meet with me to help clarify our role. The hour before they came, I blazed through the house, swiping the dust, vacuuming the floor, and picking up Sarah's toys. Sarah was napping, and Al was sleeping after his night shift. I would be by myself in this meeting.

The doorbell rang. Jackie smiled through the glass door as I opened it. She introduced me to her supervisor, Sue.

"I've heard a lot of about you." The supervisor smiled and sat on the sofa next to Jackie.

"Please, help yourself to some tea and cookies," I said. I poured myself some tea and made a beeline for our recliner. It was my space for devotions and social worker visits. I could choose to recline or rock. This choice gave me a tiny sense of control. Today, I rocked in short little bursts.

"Jackie tells me you wanted to visit about what happened the other day," Sue said as she sipped her tea daintily. "I know it was a hard day for you." She studied me over her glasses.

"Yes. Yes," I replied, stalling, trying to figure out who I was dealing with. It didn't take me long to see that I was in over my head.

"Why don't you tell me what happened, from your perspective."

I told her I hadn't meant to threaten the family support worker. It hadn't been about the worker at all. It had been about me, the mama bear who wanted to protect my young.

"One minute I am supposed to protect Sarah and the next minute I am supposed to be hands-off. I don't know what you want. Do you want me to take care of her or not?" My voice thinned out, desperate to stuff down the rising anger.

"Laurie, it's not a matter of us wanting you to take care of her. It's a matter of being more balanced. We want you to be engaged and attached but not attached in ways that keep you from being objective and rational when you need to be."

She studied me a bit and continued, "How old are you?"

"Forty-nine."

"Have you been to the doctor to get your hormones checked? You know what happens to pre-menopausal women. Their emotions get more difficult to manage."

In the space of thirty minutes, our conversation turned from the problems faced by foster parents to a mid-life woman who was a "crazed mama." I knew I couldn't win, but I wasn't one to go down without a fight.

"As I see it, we are dealing with a three-legged stool," I said. "The biological family is one leg. The system is one leg. And the foster parents are the other leg. But you sit on a stool held up by only two legs and forget about the foster parents, the third leg."

"Laurie, our agency must follow regulations given to us by the state and federal governments," Sue replied. "We are not free agents. We are part of a system. Whether we like it or not, there are just some things we have to do, including giving biological parents as many chances as possible to make some progress. That sometimes means we have to take calculated risks for their growth."

I couldn't catch my breath.

"We need our foster parents to be able to love these children but not hold them too tightly. We need you to be caring but also objective."

"I don't know how to do that." My fists, stuffed under my legs, tightened. A prize fighter, I now felt down for the count. Sarah had my heart. Objectivity was no longer an option.

"We want to help you," Sue said as she got up from the couch and clicked her heels across our wood floors in a wave of perfume and authority. "When it comes time to report on how Sarah is doing with parental visits, keep it factual. When you need to vent, just send me an e-mail with your feelings. And make that doctor's appointment."

I never did make the doctor's appointment nor e-mail Sue. Nor did I try to divorce my heart from my head. Loving a child is not an objective process. Love is not linear, factual, calculating. It is full of back roads, cul-de-sacs, dead ends, and glorious vistas. Loving cannot be regulated. It is wildly passionate, protective, stubborn, and loyal. Tell any parent she must deal in facts when she wipes poopy bottoms, reads the same book twenty-five times, searches for a favorite lost blanket for an hour, and stays up all night with a sick child!

Regarding Sarah's visits with her parents in their apartment, it took an early childhood professional outside the system to blow the whistle on the cigarette butts and dog poop on the carpet. A staff member from Parents As Teachers, a home visiting program, visited Sarah's parents in their apartment where she saw the messes. She then called the foster care agency about her concerns. Not long after, the foster care agency discontinued the home visits. And Sarah resumed parental visits with supervision at the foster care office.

We were later told that often foster parents can't always be trusted to tell the truth about their observations. So the facts reported are often judged as suspect because they may be laden with a vested interest in keeping the child. Some foster parents apparently tell bold lies so they have better chances of eventually adopting the child. Everyone knew we wanted to keep Sarah forever. But those people who knew us also knew we weren't game players or liars. We wanted to ensure Sarah's safety during visits and simply reported what we observed.

But that didn't change the fact that we did want to adopt her. At this point, their suggestion about being caring and objective at the same time felt impossible.

CHAPTER THIRTEEN

Battling Toddler

Late Spring 2008

*S*arah wasn't buying the fact that her night-night prayer signaled it was time for sleep. As she thrashed about in her crib, I lay on the floor and watched her shake her crib so hard I thought it would break. The more she cried, her face reddened and her knuckles whitened. Sarah had begun to feel safe and secure with us and was testing the boundaries. Meltdowns seemed to mean, *I know you love me. But prove it to me again.*

"I want my baboo," she screamed, calling out for her bottle. She tried a different route, knowing bottles at bedtime were off limits. "I want my baby. My baby!" More wails.

"Sarah," I shouted. "You have your baby. Here!" I pushed the white stuffed penguin, given to her by her birth mother, toward her. "Go to sleep, Sarah. Sleep!"

It seemed Sarah wanted to jump from being one to being three. For her, the terrible twos were coming early and began somewhere at the year and a half mark. Going night-night in her bed was one of those areas where she was more than willing to wage World War III. After much hair-pulling and consternation, I tried a new trick. I'd lie on the floor and not engage with her but also not leave the room. I wanted to show her I wasn't abandoning her. During the first six to eight months, I let her cry in her crib for no more than fifteen minutes before I checked on her, but rarely was a second check needed as she was sound asleep.

But that changed a few months down the road. Some nights the battle went on for as long as an hour. After a long fight, she curled up with her baby, the penguin, and wrapped her arms around its red and black scarf. The poor arctic animal was showing wear and tear. Its white body was graying and growing out of shape, and its webbed feet were peeling into tiny black pieces. The sight of that loved-off-fur penguin was what my insides were feeling like.

Sarah's light brown baby fuzz was ruffled and her checks were red, but finally, her little body, fitting snugly into her flannel pajamas, heaved up and down with sleep.

I got up from the floor, sore in body and emotions. I learned to make use of floor time by praying for all of us. Most often, I prayed God would give me the grace not to scream or run out of the room and slam the door.

"Please, God, help me be a better, calmer mother." Not that the floor torture helped me much with developing patience. I'd pray for Sarah, knowing the prolonged meltdowns could be a result of her early trauma and neglect, her fear of abandonment. That's why I stayed in her room rather than putting her down and shutting the door. The perils of foster parenting include the fact that you know so little about the past and yet need to respond appropriately to the present. This tension often left me feeling inept. I was flying blind a lot of the time.

My sister told me about a writing contest in a magazine inviting people to share stories about the "first time they felt like a grown-up." As I reflected on this, I realized watching Sarah shake the crib was an important part of my becoming an adult. It wasn't the power I had to enforce at bedtime. It was the power I had not to crush her feisty spirit but rather to love her in the midst of this meltdown. Butting heads with a strong-willed child without abusing her separates the girls from the women. For me, this signified my becoming a woman.

Bedtime was only one of many tests Sarah threw at us. Though she was only eighteen months, it seemed her terrible twos were manifested in blazing color. She was very strong-willed and bright, capable of running circles around any adult who didn't have intact boundaries. Her nature stretched us to set boundaries, and most helpful to us in setting them was the advice shared in *Parenting with Love and Logic: Teaching Children Responsibility* by Foster W. Cline and Jim Fay.

The book guides parents in setting age-appropriate boundaries. For example, when she touched the stove and we asked her to stop and she did it again, I took her to her room and sat her on her little chair for a minute. I came back after the minute to talk about what happened, hugging and kissing her and reassuring her of my love. There were times we had to repeat this process several times before the behavior stopped.

And then there were the combative diaper changes. She flailed and refused to have them changed. So then we stopped and sat down next to the changing table, watching all the time to make sure she was safe. Sometimes she lay on there for fifteen to twenty minutes before she gave in.

Increasingly it became clear Sarah needed and wanted control. Any transition was difficult for her, whether it was going from her bath to her nightie, from the car to the house, or from breakfast to her morning nap. We spent more time transitioning than doing the actual event. But the flip side of her controlling nature was her extreme brightness. She showed an emotional wisdom and mental sharpness beyond her years. It seemed that her early suffering was helping her to develop an uncanny understanding about life.

For example, she learned to pray by bowing her head and grasping our hands as is our mealtime custom. One day I forgot to pray with her, and she bowed her head anyway. She'd say "amen" by saying "men." We knew we weren't free to have her undergo formal Christian training. But we were a Christian household, and it was apparent to us she was being shaped by our spiritual practices.

She loved music. We took her to KinderMusic, a program that provided parents and toddlers the opportunity to enjoy music and movement together. She became fond of dancing to the beat, as well as humming to familiar tunes: "I Love You, You Love Me" from the Barney CD and some nursery rhymes as well as her KinderMusic tunes. She loved being read to and absorbed many books each day. She'd go into her room and play for twenty minutes, listening to her music and flipping the pages of her books as if reading to herself.

Another poignant time was when her pediatrician recommended that we set up an appointment with a cardiologist to check further on a detected heart murmur. I will never forget watching the nurse wrap her in a white sheet. It prevented Sarah from moving her arms and legs as the monitor scanned her heart. She looked like a little mummy, wrapped in the sheet with only her face and eyes exposed. She lay still as the Barney video started above her. Barney bumbled his way through the park full of kids playing on swings and slides and sang, "I love you, you love me, we're a happy family. With a great big hug and kiss from me to you. Won't you say you love me, too!"

Sarah turned to stare at Al and me. She looked so vulnerable but also so brave, so still and yet so alive. So small and yet wise beyond her years. Though she had no words, she knew how to tough out new situations. It was the courage that was born in her soul when they took her from her original home and brought her to us. It was the courage we saw in the doctor's office that day. It was that same kind of courage we saw time and time again in the days to come.

She fought diaper changes and bedtimes. But she fought much more than that. She fought the right to move forward in her little life—not only to survive but also to thrive and to grow. The doctor told us not to worry about her heart murmur. She would outgrow it. But we knew no medical science could ever do for our little family what love was doing. It was healing hearts and making champion survivors of all of us. We would survive the next months, as long as we could love.

CHAPTER FOURTEEN
Forming Family

July 2008

We were in the park.

"Come on Sarah!" shouted Addie, my great-niece who helped Sarah climb the steps to the slide. Addie put Sarah on her lap and they slid down, giggling and shrieking. Those two loved being together at summer family gatherings in Salina, Kansas, where Jane and her two daughters and their families lived.

"Way to go," shouted Caleb, Addie's big brother, as he ran ahead of the girls to show off how to *really* do it. They followed him, and the threesome ran off to play on the merry-go-round. Shawn, their daddy, pushed the multicolor merry-go-round. He nabbed Sarah, stumbled and squealed as he tickled her. "Hey, little girl, watch out!" Shan, my niece, hopped on with the happy troupe as Shawn put Sarah in her arms.

Al's brother and his family in Abilene were also some of Sarah's favorites. Every few months, we trekked to Abilene where Al's nieces and nephews, older than Caleb and Addie, treated Sarah like a little sister. Maya, Al's eight-year-old niece, took Sarah with her wherever she went. Acting like a little mother, she changed Sarah's diapers and fed her. And Sarah loved Jacoby, Maya's brother. As the family piled on their big couch to watch sports on TV, Sarah climbed onto Jacoby's lap and followed him around wherever he went. Sarah also hugged and kissed their dogs and learned their names, repeating those names as we headed home.

"So what are the names of the dogs?" Al asked as he sat next to her in the back seat. I drove into the Sunday twilight with the first stars popping out in the prairie skies.

"Barney, Hoot, Dixie, and ...?" She petered out.

"Sasha. It's Shasha," Al chimed in.

"Sasha!" She parroted Al as he handed her her blanket, Baby, and bottle.

As the sky darkened, my two loved ones fell asleep in the back seat. I marveled how quickly Sarah had become family not only to us, but also to our extended families. As she neared her one-year mark with us, increasingly her biological parents were in and out of jail, and visitation had become more sparse. It looked as if the agency would recommend parental rights be terminated. Her parents had been given multiple chances to improve, but they persisted in old patterns. Neither parent had fulfilled all the tasks required so they could get Sarah back. In late summer 2008 when Sarah had lived with us for more than a year, the foster-care agency recommended to the court that parental rights be terminated.

Kansas and federal statutes require agencies to establish permanency for a child within fifteen months of being placed in foster care custody. That means being reunified with biological parents or being adopted. Increasingly, federal and state statutes require agencies to find kinship placements for children taken out of their biological homes. If reunification with biological parents isn't possible, then extended family is considered, if appropriate, as the permanent, adoptive home.

In Sarah's case, the paternal grandfather opted for noninvolvement. The maternal grandparents asked to be considered as a kinship placement. Home studies—required before a child is placed in a home—failed for various reasons. But they continued monthly visits with Sarah at the agency office.

As the professionals slogged through months of complications, Sarah, Al, and I moved forward. Her development could not be frozen, even though everyone else—social workers, agency staff, judges, kin and the courts—seemed unable to get off square one. By now, we were her *psychological family*. This term, penned by child development specialists, describes a situation in which a child is wanted and loved by her caretakers and is bonded with them in a strong, longtime relationship.

The relationship was key, not the names we called ourselves. From the very first, we referred to ourselves as "Mommy" and "Daddy." When we'd conferred early on with social workers, no one had discouraged the practice, so that's what we settled into. As a toddler, Sarah didn't understand what *biological parents* meant though it seemed that on some level she recognized she'd been separated from her birth parents. We felt that she would forever suffer from this primal wound to some degree even though we were committed to helping her to heal by loving her and guiding her through life.

The battle between bonding and blood was cooking up with new intensity. Now a date would be set for a termination hearing. Social workers told us the court date should be set in September.

After all this reflecting on the way home from Abilene, I took a sleeping Sarah out of the car and carried her into the house and to her crib. I felt her weight against my body. Her hair, wet from being cuddled up in her blanket, matted to her forehead. I kissed her cheek and she stirred lightly. Though she was twenty-plus pounds and quite a lug, I didn't care how much longer we had to carry her on this foster-to-adopt journey. I felt that no distance would be too great. It's good we didn't know that the next part of our journey would be the longest yet.

CHAPTER FIFTEEN

Postponing Court

September 2008

Rosie, Sarah's social worker, came for her monthly visit. Sarah had lived with us for thirteen months and by now was a year and a half. Rosie plopped on the sofa and nervously fingered her pen. "Laurie and Al, the good news *was* that we had set the termination hearing date for September 15. The bad news *is* that the assistant district attorney resigned and another date has to be set. It's likely to take several months to get on the court docket again."

Al and I exchanged glances. There had been many disappointments. But this was a big one. The sooner termination happened—and it was likely to, given the lack of improvement on the part of Sarah's parents—the sooner the adoption process could begin. Anyone could apply to be her adoptive parents, and it looked like it we were not the only ones who wanted to adopt Sarah. Her maternal grandparents had also applied. The agency and the courts would have to determine which family would be chosen as her forever family.

We had been told early on that termination hearings often get postponed. Attorneys, social workers, Sarah's attorney (*guardian ad litem*) and CASA (Court Appointed Special Advocate) workers had to be in the same room at the same time. Courts are notorious for failing to find a date that fits everyone. So the hearing gets pushed farther and farther ahead on the calendar, often making the twelve- to fifteen-month open-ing for establishing permanency impossible.

I snapped back into the present. "How can an assistant attorney resign and not even tell you?" I asked.

"I'm sorry," Rosie said. "I'll keep checking and let you know as soon as I know the next date."

The younger the child, the more important it was that the fifteen-month statute be honored. Many child development experts indicate that consistency of care for children birth to five years of age is paramount. The primal wound of being taken from their original home would always remain. But the younger the child, and the sooner that child could be placed in a new forever home, the better her chance of healing. Sarah came to us at five and a half months and was never removed from us. We hoped and prayed she would be with us forever.

But this court date setback added to our stress of caring for Sarah as we also tried to meet the demands of the foster care system. Al and I were exhausted from social worker visits, parent and grandparent visitations, and living in limbo. We felt like we were in a pressure cooker. A foster family is on a merry-go-round of obligations. Rarely could we plan an agenda that simply centered around our little family. There was always some other demand to meet, some other appointment to attend, a yearly recertification process. We were not free to spontaneously drop off Sarah at the home of a friend or a family member without approval from the agency. This all added another layer of responsibility to the stresses common to usual parenting.

Repeatedly, Jackie, our social worker, recommended we find respite care for Sarah. That would allow us to take her to a family, licensed with the agency, to be cared for while we recharged our batteries as a couple. But we felt, given the amount of trauma Sarah had already experienced, that she shouldn't undergo yet more transition.

We did find some relief in a new category of care that had been created, *informal visitation*. A home selected for this care need not be licensed with the state. After a background check was positive, the home could be approved by the foster care agency as a place for Sarah to visit forty-eight hours each month to enhance her socialization. We chose the home of my sister Jane and her husband, Vaughn.

Going to their home wasn't Sarah's only new experience. She also began sessions with a play therapist. Her social worker felt this would be good for Sarah, given some of Sarah's behaviors, such as hitting, biting and kicking. These visits were so the therapist could observe her and determine what these behaviors meant. The therapist also wanted to assess how much bonding and attachment had occurred with us.

During her first visit with the play therapist, he got down on the floor with Sarah, playing with trucks, dolls, and blocks. I looked on, the proud mama. Sarah engaged easily with him and sidled up to me occasionally to ensure I was watching.

"As far as I can tell, Sarah is right on target with her development and is a bright little girl," he said. "I don't know for sure why her social worker asked that I see Sarah. There is not a whole lot I can do in play therapy with a child who is under two. But I'll continue to see Sarah as long as her social worker is recommending it."

He asked Sarah to put the toys away and turned to me. "Are you OK?" He handed me a box of tissues.

"Mommy?" Sarah looked at me quizzically and pushed into me.

"Yes. Yes. I'll be OK, somehow," I faltered. "I can't believe we are sitting here doing this. I think I need therapy more than Sarah." I gathered our things and picked up Sarah. "Thank you. Thank you so much. And, oh yes, what about that running away from us all the time. What does that mean?"

I told him about the times she had tried to run way from us. One time she ran away from us in the parking lot at the foster care agency. Another time someone saw her run from me in the parking lot of our local grocery store. That person called someone in Sarah's extended biological family, who called the agency to say she felt Sarah was unsafe in our care. Jackie, our social worker, had called to discuss this with me.

I didn't welcome the call. I explained I was juggling bags and a baby, and Sarah ran away from me in the process. As we talked, I agreed that, yes, I should have taken her to her car seat first. Yes, the baby and not the groceries were my first concern. Yes, I understood the report to be put in my file over this incident didn't mean anything other than protocol. We wouldn't have Sarah taken from us. Yes. Yes. I understood.

What I most understood was that our small city was a fish bowl. I often felt I was damned if I did and damned if I didn't. Had I reprimanded Sarah harshly in that parking lot, that person may have called to report abuse. This was conjecture, and after all, I didn't blame people for caring about her safety. Yet, I felt the pain of having failed when I was trying so hard.

The therapist broke into my thoughts. "Running away from parents is normal for toddlers experiencing the freedom of new mobility. But running so far from you, I'm not sure. It could be that she wants to test whether you love her enough to run after her and take care of her."

As I packed Sarah into her car seat and drove home, I mused more about what he said. Though Sarah did not show signs of Reactive Attachment Disorder (RAD)—a condition developed within children who are taken from caretakers and find it difficult to trust—I wondered if her running away was a thread of that condition. It seemed she was trying to prove to herself and to me that she didn't need anyone. But I felt she needed to know someone would find her, no matter how far she ran. Somehow, in God's scheme of things, the three of us had found each other a year ago. The only way we would lose each other now would be if the system decided to place Sarah with someone else. But we would have to wait agonizing months for the certainty we craved.

CHAPTER SIXTEEN

Surviving Limbo

November and December 2008

Sweat poured down my face as I wrestled to dissemble the crib—ironically the same crib Al had spent so many hours putting together. A social worker told us that at eighteen months, foster families must transition a toddler from crib to bed. Earlier, Al's brother and sister-in-law gave us a toddler bed, and now I was following the regulations.

Easy for the "rules" to say we need to do this, I thought. I unscrewed the crib, and it fell into a heap. On top of the heap were pieces of the crib with Sarah's teeth marks, reflecting her attempt to soothe her teething.

I tripped over some sharp screws. "Darn!" I yelled as I hauled the crib pieces out of the room and put the screws in a plastic baggie. I focused on the pile of unassembled toddler bed. Given her problems with transition, getting Sarah to sleep in it every night might be even more complicated.

I tried to look on the bright side. This weekend, Al had taken Sarah and his niece Maya to the wedding of a good friend. They'd left Saturday and were to return late Sunday afternoon. Our baby was growing up, and I took this rare opportunity for a trip to the store to buy some big-girl décor for Sarah's room. I came home with Tinkerbell linens and bedspread, colored in pink and purple, as well as a purple lamp and rug.

I put the toddler bed together quickly and dressed the mattress and pillow with the new sheets. For finishing touches, I laid the purple rug near the side of the bed. I turned on the light in the gathering dusk. I stepped back to view my handiwork and smiled. I hoped her new room would communicate to Sarah that mommy had missed her and had been hard at work on her behalf.

A half hour after I finished, Al drove his car into the driveway. The door screeched open, and Sarah leapt into my arms. "Mommy!" It felt strange, but so good, to have her in my arms again. I had ached to have this little person, who so exhausted me, back home. When she wasn't with me, I really missed her. It's funny how a few childless hours could so quickly turn into a void.

"Sarah, come look what Mommy did!" I took her by the hand and opened the door to her room. Her eyes grew wide as she ran to the bed and jumped.

"Look, your very own bed, and purple sheets!" I said. This purplish room made a big impression on her. From then on purple was her favorite color. Anything we bought for her—shoes, sippy cups, clothes, books— would have to be purple, if at all possible. That made for some very weird fashion ensembles.

She roamed the room, touching her new purple things, as Al came to the doorway and put his arms around me. "Sweetheart, you are too much!" We hugged and kissed. It was so good to have the family home. Sarah didn't waste time in bringing me one of her favorite books, *I'll Love You Forever*.

"Mommy, sit." She pulled me to the sofa and climbed on my lap. After separation the first thing she wanted to do was read books. I was a writer, a reader, and a highly verbal person, and she was following my love of words. "I'll love you forever, I'll like you for always, as long as I'm living, my baby you'll be," I read in singsong. Without letting me finish, she squirmed and reached for *Thomas the Train*, and we remained intertwined with words and hugs for about a half hour.

That night and many after, I realized the crib difficulty had been nothing compared with Sarah's endless schemes for not going to sleep in her toddler bed. Though she was squirrelly and combative about sleeping in the crib, at least it provided boundaries.

With her graduation to the toddler bed, bedtime would become a new world. I tucked her under Tinker Bell and hoped the fairy would touch

Sarah with sleep. I knelt by her as she wiggled under the covers and found the penguin she'd named Baby. I prayed as I did every night, "Dear Lord, please let Sarah know how much you love her and how much we love her. Please let her grow up to be the person you have created her to be."

She peeked her little face out from the covers. "Mommy, new bed. Purple. Bed!"

This was going to be a very long night. I turned off the light and lay on the floor by her bed. She climbed over the side and sat on my back. I pretended sleep. "Mommy. Mommy. Look! Bed! Purple" Still, I pretended sleep.

For the next two hours, I pulled her back into the bed and she crawled out again. It became a game for her. She roamed the room and pulled out toys from her chest of drawers and threw socks from her dresser. Still, I pretended sleep. My heart raced, and my face flushed.

"Sarah, get back to bed!" I thought my stern voice would cajole her into compliance, but no way. She continued to roam and to climb on my back. She gave me a butterfly kiss on the check and tapped my back with her hand. My emotions, as well as the room, were turning into a disaster zone.

Given the fact that we both had strong, stubborn spirits, this was a big battle. When she dumped out the last of the CDs next to her music box and put on one of them as high as the volume would go, I lost it.

"Sarah, to bed, now!" I turned on the light. Chaos. Everywhere. Clothes, CDs, books, baby dolls. All scattered on the floor as if a tornado had hit.

Sarah's final flop into bed had nothing to do with my meltdown. It probably had more to do with how exhausted she was. Finally, in a tangle of Tinker Bell, Baby, and blankets, she fell asleep.

Soon after the toddler bed transition we waited for the termination hearing to occur. It had been reset for December 8, more than three months after the original date of September 15. It turned out the judge had left only a half day on the docket to hear the case and decided he needed a whole day. So he put the court date off until mid-December. On the day of the hearing, one of the attorneys had an emergency surgery and the termination hearing was again postponed—to late March.

As the week of postponement faded into Christmas week, the golden symbol of the Baby Jesus coming into our world fell dull and brassy on our waiting hearts. We put up a tree and neatly placed packages beneath it. But our emotions felt more like Sarah's room after a nighttime battle. Hopes of timely permanency for Sarah were dashed. In the midst of a season of hope and celebration, the limbo we lived in brought feelings of powerlessness.

CHAPTER SEVENTEEN

Crossing Rapids

February 2009

I swiped my coat from the closet and hunted down my car keys. I was going to pick up Sarah, who would turn two in a week, from a grandparent visit at the agency. Al called from the bedroom, "Don't forget to tell them we don't think it's wise to schedule a family birthday party on Monday afternoon at the agency. After childcare in the morning, she needs her afternoon nap or else it's meltdown time." We had been taking her to child care a couple mornings a week to provide much-needed social connections for her, given the fact that her circle of people was tightened because of the fostering restrictions.

I opened the front door and cold air rushed in. "Don't hold your breath, Al. You know how lenient they are in letting the biological family have visits with Sarah when it fits their schedule. I doubt our schedule or opinion about her needs will count."

"Sweetheart, please don't pitch a fit with the social workers if they insist on the party. You're fighting a losing battle."

I glared at him as my pulse quickened. I could see a fight brewing. Lately we'd fought about everything. Our increasing fatigue from living in limbo took us into the ring more than usual. We turned on each other as an outlet to relieve our stress. Despite our repeated inquiries as to whether the time of Sarah's two-year-old birthday party with her family at the agency could be changed, we'd heard no verdict. This delay, though not huge in and of itself, added to my growing anger over feeling that other people disregarded our family schedule.

I got into the car and drove to the agency office. As I opened the door, Hal, the family support worker, greeted me stiffly. Usually laid back, this six-foot man looked uptight.

"Miss Laurie, my supervisor has decided to let the family have the party on Monday afternoon." He avoided my gaze and toyed with his cell phone.

"*Now* you tell us!" My voice rose. "We voiced our concerns two weeks ago about a Monday afternoon party. And then you wait until a couple of days before the party to tell us. Not only is it disrespectful to Sarah's schedule, but also to us."

Hal plead innocence. "This was not my decision. I follow orders. My supervisor felt since the judge is likely to terminate parental rights, we should allow the family some leeway."

Open-mouthed, I stared at Hal. Months of frustration left me feeling spent and used. Hal dialed his cell phone and handed it to me. "It's my supervisor. Talk to her."

I grabbed it and stomped out the door into the cold.

Without waiting for her to explain, I launched in. "What is this crap? What a great policy—letting the family do whatever it wants to do when it wants to do it! What about Sarah? What about us? You just let that family walk all over you! Where is your backbone?"

She floundered in her explanation, and I continued to lash out, unrelenting. "And you wonder why we feel like a hotel. You want us to take care of Sarah, but then you want us to be hands off. Fine, just *blanking* fine! If you have a rule book for how to do something as insane as that, I want to see it!"

My hot tears dotted the ice at the curb as our social worker, Jackie, drove up with a coworker and looked at me disapprovingly but said nothing as she went inside. I followed her inside and tossed the phone back at the family support worker.

Jackie called me into her office to calm down as another social worker retrieved Sarah from the visitation room. "Mommy!" Sarah ran down the hall and into my arms. I hid my face in her jacket, not wanting her to see my tear-streaked face.

"I'll call you next week," Jackie said. She forced a smile as I carried Sarah out to the car. I knew this thing was far from over.

† † †

Sarah turned two in the flurry of the Monday party, followed by our own party at home a couple of days later. Then came birthday fanfare at preschool. After the festivities fizzled out, and I calmed down, I realized my outburst was about lack of control. I was sliding into the abyss of our inability to keep what seemed to be Sarah's best interest in the center of the swirling maelstrom. The rights of her parents still had not been severed. The grandparents hoped to adopt. Al and I loved Sarah and weren't about to let go. And the agency professionals, charged with keeping her custody case from imploding, seemed increasingly unable to guide a flooded, raging river from overflowing its banks.

But sandbagging the shore was still part of our social worker's job. Jackie came to Sarah's monthly visit after her birthday. Sarah's social worker, Rosie, came with her, as was often their practice. We made polite conversation until Jackie got down to business.

"Laurie, it was inappropriate for you to go to my supervisor with your complaints. I've warned you repeatedly when you have problems to call me first. When we pulled up into the parking lot that day, I heard you screaming into the cell phone before I even got out of the car. That was not a good thing. Not a smart move."

"Well, I, you ... they, I mean. ...how smart is it to totally disregard ..." I was unable to finish my sentences as shame silenced me. As much as we may have been disrespected, I had disrespected them far more. I tried to cover my tracks, but they were too wide and too deep. Backed into a corner, I felt bloodied and beaten. I said out loud what had been brewing in me the past few months.

"I think we've all identified I am not good at this. After the court date is over and the decisions are made, I am pulling out of fostering. I hope like crazy we get to keep Sarah as our forever child. But after her future is resolved, I'm done."

Silence hung in the room. I gathered up my coat to leave. I felt sick to my stomach and unable to stay. "Al, you will have to finish this meeting. Good-bye."

My hands shook as I drove west out of town. The late afternoon sun glinted off patches of thin snow drifts dusted grey from traffic. I prayed for the courage to go back home. Sarah needed her mommy. Al needed reassurance. And I needed to sit down at the supper table as if family was a certain and solid rock, able to hold up under shifting sands. Our ritual of sitting down together for supper and conversation, followed by Sarah's request I read Jesus stories, never failed to comfort me after a ragged day. This evening, I needed Jesus to be more than a child's story. I needed him to heal the child within me, afraid of the people and the system that felt so big and that I allowed to make me feel so small.

Thankfully I felt the presence of Jesus after I put Sarah to bed. I lay in my bed wrapped in my worn bathrobe and curled into a fetal position. I pled for God to give me inner strength to care for Sarah in the present, no matter what the future held. I asked God to forgive my wrongs. As I prayed, God gave me a vision of Sarah clutching me as we crossed a raging river full of dangerous debris. As I fought off waves and objects to keep them from harming her, we reached the other shore. I was weary, but she was safe. I sensed God saying, "Laurie, don't focus on the objects coming at you but on getting her safely to the other side. I will deal with the dangers. You fulfill your mission."

As I stared into the dark, I prayed for a sign that all this would be OK, that all the pushing and pulling would somehow resolve in peace. God did not promise a happy ending. But I was comforted to know that God placed a child in our home and that Al and I were helping Sarah cross dangerous waters she could not have waded through alone.

CHAPTER EIGHTEEN

Bonding Strongly

March 2009

I bundled Sarah into her heavy spring jacket for a parent visit at the agency office. Her parents had fewer visits—two, rather than four a month—given the fact their parental rights were likely to be terminated. But the agency had increased the maternal grandparent visits from one to two each month as they, too, wanted to adopt Sarah. At the end of March the termination hearing would be held where more of Sarah's future would unfold.

Given all this uncertainty, I felt increasing anxiety when I took Sarah to those visits. Transporting her to visits had always produced anxiety. Months ago I had created a prayer ritual to help get us from point A to point Z. That ritual saved my sanity now. Besides being good for me, I also felt an urgency to provide as much spiritual formation in Sarah's life as I could with the time we had.

"OK, Sarah, let's pray," I looked in the rearview mirror as she clutched her new Winnie the Pooh. A few months ago we'd replaced her soiled Baby with Winnie, a new favorite since we'd played the Pooh video. I watched in the mirror as she bowed her head.

"Jesus, we ask you to be with Sarah today as she visits her family, and we ask that you let the good in and keep the bad out. Most of all, we ask that you help her to remember that you hold her tight, that you live in her heart and that you will be with her, even when we're not."

She lifted her head and asked. "Mommy, can I take Winnie the Pooh with me, too?" She busied herself with arranging his red suit and smoothing his yellow fur. She often fiddled with objects to avoid looking into my eyes and connecting with me after prayer. She avoided showing feelings and diverted herself with toys or by changing the subject.

"Sarah, look at Mommy," I smiled. "It's going to be OK. I will pick you up in two hours. And tell me again, who will be with you?"

"Jesus," she said as she unhooked the car seat and climbed out, dragging Pooh behind her. The bear was a tangible object she could see. Even if Jesus was an invisible presence, I knew she was getting it, this talk about Jesus and the heart. Though we had begun to talk to her about Jesus long ago, she was now at the age where dialogues were happening fast and furious. Her vocabulary was growing by leaps and bounds, and our conversations showed her verbal skills were racing far ahead of the two-year old norm.

The night before Sarah, as was her usual custom, asked me to read Jesus stories to her from a Bible story book a dear friend had loaned us. "OK, smuff button." I called her by my pet name and tousled her brown hair. Sarah, Pooh and I hunkered down in the recliner. We turned to one of her favorite stories about the little boy who provided the five loaves and two fish for Jesus to feed the crowds.

"Mommy, read it again," she pled. I yawned and gave it my best though I was tired. I'd have to close this reading down quick if I hoped to navigate bath and bed with energy. I closed the book and attempted to transition to the bath. Engaging with her in dialogue usually did the trick.

"Sarah, do you know who else lives in your heart besides Jesus?"

She looked at me quizzically, not sure where this was going.

"Did you know there is room in your heart for other people, too?" *I* wasn't even sure where this was going, but she seemed to be going with me.

"When people love each other, they live in each other's hearts. Daddy and I live in your heart along with Jesus, and you live in our hearts along with Jesus, too."

Her deep brown eyes seared into mine, seeming to say, *I want this to be true, but is it really? Will you always be here for me, Mommy? When will I know this for sure?*

Also without words, I gazed back to her, saying with my eyes, *Sarah, the heart is where families live. Even if you leave this house, you will always live in our hearts.*

That evening I could not tell if the heart story struck a chord with Sarah. In some ways, she kept herself well-guarded and controlled. But usually within a couple of days, she'd let us know that she heard and understood.

A few days later, I took Sarah to preschool, and we prayed our usual prayer. I asked, as I always did, "Who will be with you when I drop you off at school?"

"Jesus," she chirped.

Bingo. Right answer. I was grateful.

She gazed back at me in puzzlement followed by a peaceful expression. "But don't forget Mommy, you and Daddy live in there, too. And I live in your heart. Just think. You live in hearts. Daddy lives in hearts. I live in hearts. We all live in hearts!"

My vision blurred. Sarah was teaching me what it meant to be "Mommy." It meant that hundreds of unplanned moments, such as our discussion a couple of nights before, powerfully make or break little souls. It's those moments that the system decision-makers—as much as they strive to do the right thing—can't create. Courts can place a child within a particular family. But they can't place love in the heart. Love is what happens when people with or without blood ties are bonded by thousands of such moments, fleeting in time, but imprinted forever on a life. No one can erase them. But on the other hand, no one can create them once time has been lost.

CHAPTER NINETEEN

Growing Love

Winter 2008, Spring 2009

Sarah padded out to the living room where I sat staring out our big bay window and sipping my morning coffee. She rubbed her eyes and headed straight for the book basket, chose several favorites, and crawled onto my lap.

I pulled her into my chest and she lay her head down on my shoulder. She popped up. "Kit Kat! Tabby!" She bounced out of my lap and went searching. The cats were hiding, not ready to play so early in the morning.

We read books, waiting for Al to come home from his night shift. As we opened the last flap of her *Veggie Tales* book about the ABCs, the door squeaked open, and Sarah ran, yelling, "Daddy!" I got up to fix Al hot chocolate as he lifted her in the air and brought her down to his face. He kissed her cheek and did his woodpecker impression on her neck. *Puff-puff-puff.* She squealed, "Daddy, do a baby woodpecker." *Puff-puff-puff.* "Daddy, do a mommy woodpecker." Louder yet, *puff-puff-puff.* "Daddy, do a daddy woodpecker." Loudest of all, *puff-puff-puff.*

As they played, I brought Al's hot chocolate to the coffee table and went back to refill my coffee and pour Sarah's juice. I piled onto the couch with Al and Sarah as we enacted our morning ritual, the best part of the day for all of us.

"Ah, what a night," Al sighed. He leaned his head back on the couch as Sarah bounced on his legs. "Daddy, can I watch a movie?"

"In a minute, little one. I want to talk to Mommy a little bit."

"Ah, come on, Daddy, let's watch a movie." She pulled him off the couch as he leaned over and gave me a kiss.

"Oh, alright, kiddo." She drug him to where the TV waited for her daily educational kids' show, followed by "Winnie the Pooh" or "Thomas the Train." Al and Sarah found their spot on the couch. Soon Al snored as Sarah dangled her legs off the side of his rounded stomach. She munched on peanut butter wheat toast and grapes.

Increasingly, Al was spending more time with Sarah and sacrificing sleep because my freelance business required me to spend more time out of the home. Sarah had her favorite play places, including the bay window and our cars. Often when I came home from meeting with a client, she and Al were gazing out the bay window. It was in that spot that Al often worked with her on counting, reciting the alphabet, and sounding out words he wrote on a big tablet. They worked with her name, the names of the extended family and her pets, colors, and objects. He'd also take her to the park or to McDonald's for a chocolate shake. Afterwards, they often remained in the car so she could play with the bells and whistles.

Al always had a Sarah story or two when I got home. One day as I came in the house from church, he began laughing and launched into this story.

"Sweetheart, we were at the window when you left for church," he said, "Remember how Sarah told you to take Daddy's car, and not hers? Well, you forgot to take my car and got yours instead. She turned to me with a disgusted look, held out the palms of her hands to me, and exclaimed, 'What is she doing?'"

Then there was the time Al and Sarah went with his mother to his nephew's football game. Sarah tagged along with Maya, Al's niece, and she introduced Sarah to all of her elementary-aged friends. Al said, "Maya came up to me after the game and said, 'Uncle Al, my friends were so amazed that a two year old can talk as well as she does.'" Al beamed and then grew more serious.

"When we were in the car coming home, my mom raised her voice to me about my driving, and Sarah said, 'Grandma, are you yelling at my daddy?' Mom tried to explain to Sarah she was trying to keep me from driving too fast. Sarah didn't buy it, and said, 'Grandma Beryl, you shouldn't yell at my daddy.'"

After their many walks around the neighborhood, Al came home with stories about Sarah's endless curiosity. She asked about plants or looked up in the trees and asked about a squirrel. She spouted off her opinion about whatever they saw or asked why a flower was yellow or a bird was brown.

Pickup times at preschool also provided many Sarah stories. One day when Al brought her home, he said. "Sweetheart, you should have heard Sarah today. She went to wash her hands before we left to go home. From the corner of the room, she heard me ask the teacher how she did with her aggressive behaviors that day. Before the teacher could answer, Sarah marched up to me and said, 'Daddy, I wasn't too nice to the kids today.' Her teacher tried to look serious, but I knew she was trying not to laugh."

Sarah was also fascinated with mechanical things and tasks. She loved to watch Al mow the yard or work in the backyard. One time as Al worked on the deck, she watched intently as he screwed in loose floor boards. After asking a dozen questions about what he was doing, she picked up a screw and a second screw driver and mimicked him as best she could. Needless to say, not much deck got repaired. But their relationship-building mattered much more.

One night after we put Sarah to bed, I spooned into Al's warm body and asked, "Al, what do you like most about being Sarah's daddy? You two spend so much time together, and you are getting so close."

"It is an honor to be Sarah's dad," he said as our togetherness wrapped us into tender conversation. "She has given me so much more than I have given her. I get such a warm feeling when she looks into my eyes and waits for me to give her security and answers. I get the feeling she isn't looking for something big, just something simple—someone to be there with her, someone to listen to her little stories."

"Honey," I whispered, "What will you do if she leaves us?"

A chill seeped into our shared warmth. His body stiffened. "It will leave a hole in my heart. I don't know what I will do if I lose the gift of watching her grow and change daily. It's a beautiful thing. But if she does leave, I will never stop loving her. I will always want her to be a part of our lives, in whatever way feels most comfortable to her."

I sighed as I curved into Al more tightly. My tears wet his back. Their daddy-daughter relationship had blossomed and grown. To uproot that growth would leave a hole in our hearts that could never be filled in the same way.

SECTION THREE

Releasing Sarah

Psalm 139:7–12 (NRSV)
Where can I go from your spirit?
Or where can I flee from your presence?
If I ascend to heaven, you are there;
If I make my bed in Sheol, you are there.
If I take the wings of the morning
and settle at the farthest limits of the seas,
even there your hand shall lead me,
and your right hand shall hold me fast.
If I say, "Surely the darkness shall cover me,
and the light around me become night,"
even the darkness is not dark to you;
the night is as bright as the day,
for darkness and light are alike to you.

CHAPTER TWENTY

Fearing Loss

March 2009

On Monday, a few days before the termination hearing was scheduled in court, Al called as I was driving home from taking Sarah to child care. "Sweetheart, you need to come home!" Usually calm, the panic in his voice frightened me. "They want to take her. They are going to take her!"

"Al, Al, what are you saying? What is going on?"

"Rosie, our social worker from the agency, called. The grandparents and their lawyer are trying to get the judge to agree to let Sarah live with them even before court is held. That means they could come today, and she would be gone."

"Oh, no!" I pulled into the driveway. Al was waiting. I fell into his arms. "How can they do this?" I asked.

"I don't know, sweetheart, but they are trying. Rosie will call as soon as she hears something more."

An hour later, Rosie called and said she hadn't yet heard if the judge would grant this recent request. But in a few hours she would know more. In those few hours we made frantic calls to close friends and family. We didn't want to be alone in this crisis.

The doorbell rang and Ann, our CASA worker, stood at the doorstep.

"Come in," my voice wavered.

"Laurie and Al, I am so sorry about this, but I am doing all I can to stop it," she said, attempting to comfort us. "I don't think legally they can pull this off."

Al and I held each other.

"But they're trying, and there is nothing, nothing we can do about it," I cried. "When will this all stop? When will I stop feeling so powerless?"

"I know, Laurie, this has been a long ordeal, and I want it to be over too, for Sarah's sake, for your sake." Ann placed a reassuring hand on my shoulder. "I can't stay, but I wanted you to know that there are many social workers who don't agree with this. I will do all I can."

Soon after she left, Rosie called and reassured us no action could be taken today. It seemed this was a false alarm. But she would call us in the morning to let us know for sure.

Saved from the unthinkable for at least one more day, we picked up Sarah from child care and drove to Salina to be with my sister, brother-in-law, and extended family. Jane ordered pizza and put on the coffee. As we sat around the table, family asked us questions we could not answer and shook their heads in disbelief.

Sarah played with Addie and Caleb. I hoped it was a diversion from all the anxiety. It was hard to tell how much of our uncertainty she absorbed. But child development professionals say kids absorb a lot, even before they have the capacity to express themselves in words. Because their reasoning capacities and verbal skills are not fully developed, their experiences and feelings can reside in the closets of their subconscious. When they are able to do the cognitive work regarding what is in their hearts, those closets open.

Our fears about the possibility of Sarah being taken the next day and our worries about how this experience might affect her nearly overwhelmed Al and me. The best we could do was to love her with all our hearts, just as we had all along.

I desperately wanted to hold her so tightly that no one could pry her loose. History is littered with stories of terrible scars people have suffered when others in power take them from their loved ones without notice. Our story would not make the history books or parallel the horror of such incidents. But the possibility of losing Sarah created terror in us.

† † †

The next day Rosie called to tell us the judge would not allow the family and their lawyer to proceed with the plan to take Sarah from us so quickly. The court date would go on as planned in three days. We wept with relief.

The morning of court my sister and niece Addie came over to watch Sarah; Al slept because he had worked the night before. He decided not to go to court because he did not want further emotional upset. But I wanted to hear every last word. No matter what the verdict regarding parental rights, I relished the power that came from knowledge. I finally would be privy to family information the agency had not been able to legally share with us.

To many people's surprise, Sarah's birth parents, who had been adamant about fighting to keep Sarah, relinquished their rights on their own accord. So a court hearing of this magnitude that typically takes a day or two lasted an hour. The court room was packed, as people who worked with the biological family—agency social workers, lawyers, PAT and CASA professionals, and child care staff—had come to testify. They were required to share professional opinions on whether parental reunification was in Sarah's best interests. We had been told by various agency staff that their recommendation would be to terminate rights and that the judge would certainly comply.

The surprising turnabout from the parents, who had been combative for most of the twenty months Sarah had been in our care, left many of us stunned, but relieved that an extended battle was averted. The judge dropped the gavel to end court and all of us left.

Their decision to give up their rights to Sarah was dizzying enough. But additional directives evoked a vertigo that sent me spinning emotionally for days to come.

"Laurie, now that this has happened, grandparent visits have to increase," said Rosie, Sarah's social worker, when we left the courtroom.

"Why?" I looked at her stunned. "Why now?"

"Laurie, I can't talk more now. But I will call you next week about their visits."

I walked to my car, feeling confused and afraid. A person approached me. "Laurie, I am sorry for all you're going through," she said. "Have you heard of KLS?"

"KLS? What's that?" I asked, looking at her quizzically.

"Kansas Legal Services. It is a United Way-funded agency that provides free legal services for families. A KLS attorney helped us during a prolonged custody battle, and we have since adopted our foster child."

I jotted down the phone number for KLS on a piece of scratch paper as I looked into her concerned eyes. "Thank you, oh, thank you."

Once I got home, I decided to wait on the KLS calls. Instead, I called Ann, the CASA worker, to clear up some confusion about what happened in court. She explained to me what was likely to happen now. In the twenty months we had had Sarah, two kinship placement studies were conducted with her maternal grandparents. Both times, the agency determined there were some outstanding issues that needed to be cleared up before Sarah could visit them in their home or be placed in their care.

But the week before court, the agency had cleared their home and their family as a fit adoptive placement. This meant the agency would now allow Sarah to visit the grandparents in their home and also to visit more frequently. The agency procedures required social workers to ensure that grandparents and Sarah had as many opportunities as possible to bond and attach.

Most importantly, all of these new steps meant that a best-interest staffing would be conducted. In this meeting professionals involved with Sarah's case—her agency social workers, the CASA professional, and Sarah's lawyer—would discuss the strengths and needs of Sarah and of both families. The professionals would then recommend the best adoptive family.

By now, nearly two years had passed, far beyond the twelve- to fifteen-month window allowed to agencies to resolve custody cases with young children. Given this time frame, the agency needed to schedule the best-interest staffing as soon as possible. However, we knew this could take weeks or even months.

In our prayers we asked God for a quick resolution to this long journey. But if it couldn't be quick, we at least wanted enough light to chart our next step. On this journey tall cliffs rose from both sides of the path. On one side was the horrific thought of losing Sarah. On the other side was the amazing gift of keeping Sarah in our forever family.

CHAPTER TWENTY-ONE

Brewing Storm

April and May 2009

I shuffled through the pile on my desk and found the number to call KLS. A receptionist answered and took our name and phone number as I explained the situation. She would give the information to the attorney who handled such cases, who would call back.

In a few minutes, my cell phone rang, and I carried it down to the basement so I wouldn't be within Sarah's earshot.

After I gave the initial description of what had gone on—including how long Sarah had been in our care, the relinquishment of the parents, and the wishes of the grandparents to adopt—she replied. "Oh, we handle cases exactly like yours. In fact, we specialize in them. Here's what we need to do." My heart raced. Would we get some help in navigating our way through the weeks ahead? I had no way of knowing what those weeks would bring, but according to our new attorney, they could be grisly.

For starters, the social workers insisted that grandparent visits needed to increase and be held in their home rather than at the office. Since their adoption study passed, there was no barrier to Sarah visiting there. Visits increased from two times a month for two hours each time to two times a week for four hours each time. What a huge change for Sarah and us.

The first few longer visits pumped more anxiety into our home. The first day Sarah came home from a four-hour visit, she was twitchy, restless, and inconsolable for the remainder of that evening. From what we knew about bonding and attachment, her demeanor most likely had nothing to do with the quality of the visit but of the new anxieties it piqued.

"Do you want to go downstairs and watch *Finding Nemo*?" Al asked as she wandered around upstairs, rushing into her room and then rushing out again. Al went into her room to give her some company, but that provoked a tantrum. I left them to negotiate and drove to Dillons to get Chinese takeout. When I got back, the mood was tense. Often Sarah and Al sat together on the couch. Tonight, she sat far away from him, twined instead around Pooh and another baby doll. She stared into space and then back to the television. I felt helpless so I went into the kitchen to fix plates of supper. I knew that munching food and watching a movie was about as good as it was going to get tonight.

The movie was about a little fish getting lost from his daddy and wandering far into the ocean and the journey his father took to find him. I gobbled chocolate ice cream and wondered, *Just how far out into the ocean was our journey going to take us? And what dangers existed for Sarah?* Al and I would find some adult resources to survive, but what about Sarah? How would she come through the trauma that child development specialists predict when a child is removed from a long-term caregiver? One thing I knew for sure: Just like Nemo's dad, we would go to any length and suffer great cost to ensure Sarah would incur as little wounding as possible.

† † †

That evening I was hopeful Al and I would find good coping mechanisms, but the next weeks brought new fear. As we waited for the best-interest staffing to occur—it had been scheduled for six weeks after the relinquishment—we became increasingly frightened and turned on each other.

One night for his break at work, Sarah and I took Al a Sonic hamburger, fries, and Diet Coke. Instead of having a happy time, Al and I continued a fight we had begun earlier about money, schedules, and child rearing. He had picked up extra shifts for the extra money we needed. But he also provided more care at home for Sarah as I searched for new freelancing business. It seemed we were spinning around like a gerbil on a wheel, relentlessly striving but ending up in the same place of uncertainty and little sleep.

"Why don't you look for another job!" I barked as Sarah bustled around us, getting more anxious as she sensed the mounting tension.

"We've been through this a million times, Laurie," he said. He threw his hands up, gritted his teeth, and stomped his feet. "It's never enough, is it!"

He threw the Diet Coke down on the lawn outside the offices. He banged his fist on the office door. By this time, Sarah was climbing in and out of the back seat, trying to ignore us.

"You keep doing the same darn thing and wait for a different result!" In the wake of my wrath, Al stood in the light of the parking lot lamp, his head bowed.

"Daddy, Mommy!" By this time, Sarah was scared and unsure. As was our custom, we called for a group hug for damage control. As I picked up Sarah and placed her between Al and me, I eyed Al but he wouldn't look at me. Shame, anger, and fear covered his face like a cloud. I tried to break through the cloud, but the storm had wrought its damage.

"It's OK, Sarah; it's going to be OK," he said. "I have to get inside." He hugged her but turned to go without hugging me.

"Honey," I asked, "is it going to be OK?"

Sarah tugged at my shorts. "Come on, Mommy, let's go home," she whined.

"Honey, it's going to be OK, isn't it?"

"Yes, sweetheart, yes," he said flatly.

"Al. I'm so sorry."

"So am I," he said as he bent down to kiss Sarah. She and I walked to the car and I put her in the car seat. Al disappeared inside the building.

† † †

When we got home, I struggled to get Sarah into the bathtub. "No, Mommy," she squealed as she ran into the living room. I rushed after her, my anger mounting over the stress of having to be the adult when

I had no confidence that maturity was anything I could come up with this evening.

"Sarah!" I shouted, rushing after her into the bedroom. "Fine. Don't take a bath. Don't get out of your poopy diapers. Don't go to bed and don't expect me to tuck you in!"

She stopped and stared, wide-eyed, confused. I fell onto her bed in a heap. There was no way to take back the hurt I had caused. She came to my side and stroked my back, heaving with emotion. I turned my face to hers.

"I'm so sorry, Sarah. Daddy and I love you so much. Do you know that? Do you really know that? We will always love you, no matter what we say and do."

She bent down and gazed into my reddened eyes. "I know, Mommy. I know. I will always love you, too." She stroked my arm as she sat still.

We hugged for a long time. As I always told Sarah, life is full of choices. We all must pick and choose. Obviously, my choices for the evening had been terrible. But because of the unconditional love and grace of a toddler, I knew I could be forgiven.

She took her bath peacefully, and we transitioned to her bed, but I knew Sarah was remembering my words.

Please God, grant us mercy, I prayed silently as Sarah turned away from me and curled into a ball. "Sarah, please forgive me, I want to do better," I lay next to her and gazed into the very dark room. Slowly, her body uncurled and inched closer.

"Do you want to sing, Sarah?" I began. "Hush little baby, don't say a word, Mama's gonna buy you a mocking bird. And if that mocking bird won't sing, Mama's gonna buy you a diamond ring. And if that diamond ring turns brass, Mama's gonna buy you a looking glass. And if that looking glass gets broke. …"

"Mommy, my back. My back." That was my cue. I gently rubbed and scratched her back as she settled into an uneasy sleep. I continued to sing softly to soothe my rattled nerves. "And if that looking glass gets broke, Mama's gonna buy you a billy goat. And if that billy goat falls down, you'll still be the sweetest little baby in town."

Her breathing slowed. I peered into the darkness of the room and the darkness of my heart. So many things had broken, so many things had fallen. And yet, still deep in our hearts, there was a mockingbird singing a song of hope. Sarah's sweet wisdom and God's sweeter grace wiped the slate clean and made way for another day of our forever family to thrive.

CHAPTER TWENTY-TWO

Holding On

July 2009

We wheeled Sarah down the aisles of Wal-Mart in Billings, Montana, the site of the wedding of my niece Megan. We'd flown to Billings with my elderly father and were staying at a hotel with the extended family. It was colder than in Kansas, and we had not come prepared. We wove through the aisles, looking for a very specific sweatshirt. It had to be purple, Sarah's favorite color. It had to be inexpensive. And it had to be one she liked.

This was also the week we expected to receive monumental news. While the agency had decided to choose us as the adoptive parents for Sarah, we were waiting to hear of the administrators' decision regarding the maternal grandparents' appeal. Ann, the CASA worker, asked us if we wanted to get a call from her regarding the decision when we were away on family vacation. We told her we wanted to know immediately, no matter what.

Ann and our attorney hoped we would ultimately be chosen as the adoptive parents. So many factors led them to believe it could happen. We began caring for Sarah at five and a half months. She had bonded and attached to us. She was growing by leaps and bounds in her development. And because of the trust the three of us shared, we were most equipped to help her with transition issues. Though her maternal grandparents had blood and biology on their side, we had the bonding, an increasingly important component of providing a home that met her best interests.

With all of that in our favor, there had been increasing, though subtle, signs that the administrators did not see this as a cut-and-dried case. Our attorney continued to balance our hopes with the reality that the best interest decision might award Sarah to the maternal grandparents, despite her length of time in our care.

Sarah's squeals broke into my thoughts, and she brought back my mind back to Wal-Mart. "Mommy, I want a purple one!" We had found a rack of sweatshirts her size, and I barely heard the cell phone ring over the sound of her glee.

"Hi, Laurie, this is Ann. Is Al there? Can I talk to him?" My blood froze. This could only mean one thing.

I handed the phone to him as my hand shook. "CASA."

"Hello?" he half asked, half answered. "Oh." He leaned against a clothes rack and his face drained of color. "When did they decide this? Yesterday. Why?" He listened as she answered him with the little information she had. "OK. We'll wait for you to call again. Just let us know what's next."

He hung up and handed me the phone. "They reversed the best interest decision," he said as he stared at the floor, holding back the tears.

"You have got to be kidding," I said, feeling dizzy, sick, and beaten. "Why?"

"I don't know, sweetheart, I don't know."

"This can't be possible," I said, searching to make sense of it. "What now?"

"We wait for Ann to get more information back to us."

Robotically, as if sleepwalking, we found a purple sweatshirt and kept Sarah happy as we went to search for my dad in the golf aisle.

"Dad, we have bad news," I fell into his arms. "They have reversed the decision."

"Oh, my." Dad looked from me to Al to Sarah and back again. "What now?"

"We have to wait for Ann to call back and give us more information," I said. Shell-shocked, we headed to the counter to pay for Sarah's sweatshirt.

† † †

The rest of the day we shared our news with my extended family and sat together in a daze. During the afternoon and evening Al and I called friends and his side of the family to share our news.

The following day we got ready for the mid-afternoon wedding at the home of my sister Paula and brother-in-law Mac. The day turned out sunny and warm, a perfect day for a backyard wedding. As I watched Megan walk down the grassy aisle, I remembered how I played with her when she was about Sarah's age. One Christmas vacation we discovered a Muppet tape that was good for dancing. Megan was enthralled with ballerinas so I danced with her across the living room floor, lifting her high and setting her down as if she were a ballerina on New York's Carnegie Hall stage.

How did we get from that to this? I pondered during the ceremony as Sarah wiggled and squirmed until niece Shan took Sarah to sit with her in a back row. Since we had received the call from Ann two days ago, Sarah had been mirroring and parroting the turbulent emotions swirling through our extended family. I grabbed Al's hand as I grieved the possibility of not having the honor of watching Sarah grow. Our little girl would someday turn into a woman, might take a man's hand, and walk into her own future. And we may not be there.

That night on the dance floor at the reception, I grabbed Sarah and whirled her around until sweat poured down my face and back and her glee tired her. I wanted to dance like this forever, mother and daughter, safe and trusting in the circle of holding and being held. I tried to dance out my grief, immeasurable and mute.

At one point, Al joined us and we held Sarah between us, moving to a slow dance. We held onto her, unable to fully grasp what it would mean to break the embrace and blow through the wind of separate futures.

† † †

As if the initial shock from Ann's phone call wasn't enough to put us under, little did we understand we would have to make imminent, grueling decisions about our response to this chain of events. Two days after the wedding, we returned home about midnight. We pulled Sarah's purple sweatshirt from her limp body and put her in bed. We set her sweatshirt on the table between us and stared at each other.

"Honey, the attorney is prepared to file an appeal to the administrator's decision," I said as I put my head in my hands. "But I don't know if I can take anymore. And is this good for Sarah, to continue to keep her in limbo? We have suspected other people haven't kept her best interests at heart. If we prolong this, are we just as guilty?"

Travel weary and broken, I wanted this nightmare to be over. The unthinkable had happened and what else could we do? When the bomb falls, there usually is nothing left to do but pick through the rubble left behind. Emotionally, parts of us, once intact, hopeful and earnest about doing the right thing, had imploded.

"Sweetheart, we've come this far," Al said. "We can't stop now. If we don't appeal this decision and take this all the way, she will one day come back to us and ask why we abandoned her, why we gave her up."

I knew my husband had dug in his heels. Steady, loyal to the end, and very stubborn, he was not going to let go of Sarah, who had become our little girl for life, if only in our hearts. Plus, he had that amazing gift of being unselfish and servant-hearted when the fires of suffering blazed highest. I, on the other hand, had more of a selfish side, sometimes unwilling to go that extra mile when the heat was on.

I grabbed the limp sweatshirt and held it up to my face, smelling Sarah. The purple cotton turned wet as I mourned this fork in the road. I feared that our appeal, if filed, could eventually lead to the abandonment of our dreams of family. I rocked back and forth, my head buried in her sweatshirt, smelling of Sarah and blazing with purple—the color that signified royalty and the riches of love she had given us.

As Al starred blankly to the floor, I submitted to his heart, so fixed on doing right by Sarah at all costs. "OK, honey." I felt the prolonged uncertainty our appeal would evoke was like waiting for the guillotine, but I too wanted her best more than my own comfort. The next day we called our attorney and asked her to file the appeal.

CHAPTER TWENTY-THREE

Forgiving "Adversaries"

September and October 2009

I sat across from Sister Helen Prejean, author of *Dead Man Walking*, which later became an Academy Award-winning movie in the mid-1990s. She had traveled the globe to advocate against the death penalty and had come to Kansas to speak to the Mennonite community for a weekend. A Mennonite client asked me to write a story about her, and I met her for lunch.

This interview occurred in September, about a month before the final court date, when the judge would hear our appeal and render his final decision. The decision had been reversed at the end of July. But the next available court date wasn't until mid-October. After this court date, there would be no more appeals. It was truly the fork in the road that would determine the fate of Sarah and the two families who loved her.

I had come to interview Sister Prejean, but instead, the topic turned to me.

"So, Laurie, tell me about you." Her twinkling eyes focused on me, and her rapt attention teased out my story. As my tale unfolded, I fought back the tears. *What was I doing?* I was supposed to retrieve her story, not tell my own.

At the end of my story, Sister Helen's gaze and words, though gentle, cut like a razor into my soul. "Have you ever thought that you could be friends with your foster daughter's grandmother, rather than her adversary?"

Her question jolted me. "Well, no."

Through the months the grandparents and Al and I had pulled apart and became suspicious of each other. Over the bump and grind of months of uncertainty, we had forgotten how to assume positive intent. And the intent of both parties truly was to love and cherish Sarah. Sure, we had our adult needs woven into the mix, but still, bottom line, we all loved Sarah and wanted to raise her as our own. A lot of mistakes had been made. But in the center of our hearts, we knew Sarah would pay the biggest price. In the midst of gaining a forever family, she would lose the possibility forever of being shaped by the other set of parents.

Sister Helen broke into my reflection. "Of course, you didn't think about being her friend," she said with comforting compassion. "You were in the middle of the pain. The courts are going to do what they are going to do. But you have the power to choose to love and forgive, rather than to be bitter." And then she cited the biblical story in Matthew about making friends with your enemy on the way to court.

Oh, how I wished those words had come from anyone other than Sister Helen, who had given spiritual direction to death row inmates and witnessed six deaths by state execution. If anyone was clear about forgiveness and justice and suffering, it was her. She wasn't someone I could blow off. I could not brush aside this radical messenger. God had used her to speak the truth in love.

I told her later, "Sister Helen, you ruined my weekend!" She raised her eyebrows, surprised by my outburst. I explained. When someone invites us to walk with Jesus straight through the heart of injustice experienced personally, the cost of doing so can be high. But I knew that if God had gone to all the trouble of sending someone hundreds of miles to speak to me, then I should listen. And most radical of all, I should act.

On the few days following the weekend interview, I made short work of carrying out the mission I felt God had given. After I helped Sarah out of her car seat for another grandparent visit, I made a beeline to the grandfather.

"I've been giving a lot of thought to what we've all been through," I said as I met his gaze, skeptical though curious. "You didn't ask for this, and neither did we. Even though the situation has tended to make us think we were enemies, we can choose not to be. I am sorry for any pain we've caused you the last couple of months."

"We'll be OK," he said, his back stiffening, but his eyes softening as he helped Sarah into his car. I watched in my rearview mirror as she settled down into the seat with Winnie the Pooh and waved good-bye. I waved but ducked my head. I didn't want her to see that once again, Mommy was crying.

As I drove across town, I thought about what just happened. As weird as it was, I had taken a tiny step of reconciliation in the long journey of temptation to seek revenge.

There could be no win-win. Someone would get Sarah; someone would not. She was given to our world by her Creator as a gift, not a possession. But reality was: She had the blood of kin in her veins and two-plus years of bonding with us in her heart. It was up to the judge to determine whether blood or bonding would trump.

† † †

"I call my first witness, Laurie Robinson, the foster mother of Sarah," our attorney said as I got up from my chair and approached the bench to be sworn in. I noticed the eyes of the judge, kind and warm, as he smiled to put me at ease. I knew this was a do-or-die day, and true to form, I was not going down without a fight.

"So when was the first time you felt you bonded with Sarah?" our attorney asked.

"The first time I laid eyes on her," I said without hesitating. The memory of first meeting Sarah flashed through my mind. I felt a first rush of mother love the second I met her. I could never explain that rationally. Mother love is not something rational. It embodies the mystery of how God created mothers. We are like mother bears, fiercely protecting our cubs at all costs. We are hopelessly unconditional, ready to defend our young. We are possessive, holding on to our children even when to do so means our hearts will break.

"Tell me about the nature of your relationship with Sarah," she continued.

"When Sarah first came to our home, it was more about me than about her," I said. "I wanted to be a mom. Al and I married late in life and weren't able to get pregnant. But after several months, it became more about Sarah. I thought less and less about my desire to be a mother and more and more about her needs."

"Tell me more about how you met her needs," the attorney persisted.

"Well, while all children have meltdowns, Sarah had more than her share, especially when transitioning. She couldn't go from the car into the house, from the bathtub to her changing table, or from breakfast to preschool without dawdling, messing around, fighting us all the way. She also had more than her share of emotional needs and anxieties. She tested us continually. We tried to provide good boundaries, modeling guidance from books such as *Love and Logic*. We loved her unconditionally. Our favorite family rituals were praying together at meals and bedtimes and having family hugs. We put Sarah between us and hugged her tight, reaffirming our love for her and for each other."

After a few more questions, our attorney called Al to the stand. She asked, "If you suspected Sarah was in danger when she was away from your home, would you stand up for her rights? Would you be willing to protect her?"

"Yes ma'am," Al said.

The attorney continued. "You know that if you are awarded custody of Sarah, you will not receive a stipend of any kind from the state. Since this would be a direct placement—a placement not agreed to by the agency—then you would be off the books entirely. Are you willing to provide for Sarah's needs? Do you have the ability to provide insurance and other resources?"

"Yes ma'am," he said.

"No further questions at this time, your honor," our attorney said as she sat down.

The attorney for the grandparents called a string of witnesses to the stand, most notably the administrators who reversed the decision to place Sarah with us. The attorney's questioning probed whether the agency had followed protocol on finding permanency for Sarah. He also asked why they determined placing Sarah with kin would be in her best interests more than allowing her to remain with us.

The witnesses cited their degrees and years of experience and also studies that showed children did best when placed with their extended family. No specifics were cited as to when those studies were done and by whom. Also not cited were any qualifiers as to how much time should be allowed to elapse before a child was returned to kin.

Many child development specialists are adamant that the younger the child, the more important consistency is with primary caregivers. Removing a child from a long-term family situation during birth to five years of age has dramatic ramifications on brain development. This disruption damages their sense of security and traumatizes them. The more secure their attachment is to caregivers, the freer they are to develop their capacities. These include the ability to develop language, emotional maturity, gross and fine motor skills, self regulation, connection with others outside the family circle, obedience to authority and trust that the world is a safe and good place.

Knowing all this, our attorney hit the time-element issue head-on during her questioning of agency administrators.

"And just how soon do you think it would have been appropriate to return Sarah to her kin? After two months, four months, six months, a year?"

"Well, it depends," said one of the administrators who had overturned the best interest decision. She attempted to explain why so much time had been allowed to elapse in this case—including court delays, some uncertainty within the agency as to how to sort through complications and to make the right decisions, the many families involved. None of the three administrators who overturned the decision had ever met Sarah, her biological family, or Al and me. They had not been privy to the hundreds of hours of interaction the agency staff had had with us. In essence, they had overturned the decision made by their staff most involved in the case.

Despite their lack of direct involvement, the three administrators had a total of 60 years of experience and many prodigious degrees. They also could prove they had followed state and federal procedures. They had completed tasks needed in seeking a placement for Sarah. And because they had not veered from the rule of law or their obligations, no one legally could disqualify their decision.

But tending to the spirit of the law was a different matter. Our attorney and Sarah's attorney strove to convince the judge that Sarah's best interests would not be served following the letter of the law. They would not be served by giving preference to blood. The age-old pendulum that had swung wildly through the centuries was also swinging through this courtroom. On one end of the pendulum was giving total rights to families and none to foster parents who wanted to adopt. On the other end, biological families were not given due consideration.

Could the system truly be child-centered in the way children perceive time? Could it look at this from her point of view? Or, would it be family and system centered, trying to fulfill other agenda, all the while cloaking it in the language of "best interests"?

Though laws had attempted to bring the pendulum to center, the attitudes, often hidden within communities, were that children were the property of their biological families. And unless one could prove blatant harm or prove that the child would not be cared for in basic ways, many judges were still sending children back to kin.

It was clearly documented in all the paperwork, social worker reports, and professional reports that it would do damage to Sarah to remove her now. We had become her psychological parents, she our psychological child. To remove her after more than two years in our home would devastate her entire world, which included her home, extended family, neighborhood, church, pets, friends, school. Given her problems with transition, doing this now was likely to be traumatic and damaging for a lifetime.

But as the administrators cited studies about the importance of kin, they attempted to hammer home the idea that Sarah, in the long term, would be best served by being with her biological family. No matter how much time had elapsed, she could adjust. And because she had bonded so well with us, she could transfer that bond to her grandparents.

A few more comments were made regarding the state of her grandparents' lives, but they weren't called to the stand.

"Thank you all for your participation, professionalism, and expediency," the judge said as the case closed. "It is clear to me that Sarah is more fortunate than many children. She has two families who love her and want to care for her. Because I need to reflect more upon this case and do more study, I will make my decision and render it in writing within two weeks."

I felt like a deflated balloon as we walked out of the courtroom and to the circle of our family and friends who had been sitting outside the courtroom, praying for us. As we walked outside the building, I saw Sarah's grandfather hold Sarah's grandmother as she cried. In that moment, I remembered my last conversation with her. I had approached her just as I had the grandfather and asked her forgiveness for all the pain I may have caused in this process.

In doing so, she released a litany of grievances so deep and so long that I didn't think I would be able to handle all I was hearing. She shared with me how painful it had been to watch other people raise her grandchild and how cut off she had felt in not being able to see Sarah more. In that recent incident, and now again in this moment, I knew that what had held us apart as women and mothers was only an illusion. We were simply two hurting women who wanted to be Sarah's mother and would fight to the end for that right.

I took a deep breath and approached the truck where I motioned for the grandmother to roll down her window. I reached inside and took her hand.

"It's going to be OK soon," I said, compassion rising up from the ruins of fatigue, fear, and potential loss. She looked at me with sad, frightened eyes and remained silent. As strange as it seemed, I half believed that would be true, even if Sarah were taken from us. By "OK" I meant that no matter what the judge decided, this inferno of endless anxiety and waiting for the worst to happen would be over. In no longer than ten days, we would know for sure.

And today, the final court hearing was over. I could see a light at the end of the tunnel. Whether it was clear sky or the headlight of an oncoming train, I wasn't sure, but I could see a light.

CHAPTER TWENTY-FOUR

Facing Fate

Late October 2009

Al walked in the door at 7:45 A.M. after his night shift. He was deeply troubled.

"Honey, what is wrong?" I asked, knowing it was not good. We'd been waiting for a call regarding the judge's decision. I wondered if his worries were linked to that.

"The judge awarded Sarah to the grandparents," he said as he flopped into the couch, dazed and shaken. "Someone at work had heard the news from the grandparents. Apparently the judge sent out a memo late yesterday afternoon, and the grandparents' lawyer received it." We later discovered the judge sent a fax to our attorney's office, but she had gone home for the day and didn't get it until the next morning. That's why we hadn't received a call from her.

He put his face in his hands. Tears dribbled through his fingers. I held him.

"But why didn't you come home? Why didn't you call me?" I cried. I couldn't imagine what it had been like for him to work the night through.

"I didn't want you to have to be alone with this news," he said as we clutched each other in our misery. I was thankful Sarah was sleeping late, allowing us to make calls to our families. I left for a moment to call my sister.

"Jane?" I broke down and could not talk. She listened to my weeping, knowing the verdict before I announced it. "They are going to take her. The judge ruled she should go to her grandparents. I … I don't know how to do this. How am I going to do this? There is no instruction kit for how to love a child for more than two years and then to lose her within thirty days. How will I be Mommy in this situation? She will never understand."

My worst fear had come true. We would lose Sarah, and she would think we were abandoning her. She would not understand that a judge ruled she should leave the only parents and only home and life she could remember. I pled to God for mercy even though I felt as if God had abandoned us too. How could a good God, who is all-powerful, all-loving, all-knowing allow this loss? If God were all powerful, he could have led the judge to make a different decision. If God were all loving, he would not want us to suffer like this. If God were all-knowing, he would have prevented us from marching, well-intentioned and hopeful, into the abyss of a broken system that impaled us on its jagged edges. The miscalculations and decisions of well-meaning but imperfect social workers and administrators—all required to follow a legal path that sometimes did not lead to the most sane conclusion—were impacting dozens of lives within two extended families.

Most importantly, it would impact Sarah forever. She was not a case study on a legal document. She was not a possession to be bought and sold like a car. She was a flesh-and-blood person. The system could legislate where she lived. But it could not heal her heart, soon to be broken for a second time. She was taken from birth parents when she was five and a half months. And she would be taken from her psychological parents when she was two and a half. Sarah's losses seemed more than any adult could sustain without major therapy and lifelong scars. I felt a world that requires children to undergo this wounding and to believe that because they are so young and supple that they will adjust was a world that had lost its bearings.

Those thoughts flashed through my mind that morning, for the rest of the day, and for weeks to come. I asked *why* repeatedly to family, friends, and community folks who flooded us with food, comfort, cards, and prayers. It was as if someone had died. In a sense, that was true. Something had died—the opportunity to nurture a child into adulthood, to watch her grow, blossom, flower. The vine of our intertwined lives felt stripped.

Sarah finally awoke and came out to the table where we sat, looking for her morning dose of hugs, reassurances, and book time. She took one look at us and cried, "Mommy? Daddy? What's wrong?" We tried to reassure her that we were sad but that everything was going to be OK. She wasn't buying it, and the next minutes were filled with anxious hugging and gazes into our eyes as she searched for the truth.

The doorbell rang an hour after Al delivered the news to me. Ann, our CASA worker, stood outside. The late October wind, laced with a heavy cold rain, splattered both of us as she stepped inside. The trees were flailing and writhing, mirroring the angst and devastation I felt.

I fell into her arms.

"I am so sorry," she cried as she held me.

"I don't know how to do this. How are we going to do this?" I asked.

She led me to the kitchen table and sat down with Al and me as one after another swiped Kleenexes out of the box and searched in vain for answers. We talked about next steps, about what the next month would look like. Sarah would not be with us longer than thirty days. We did not want to elongate anyone's misery. Ann would confer with the agency social workers and get back to us.

In a couple of days, a plan emerged. Sarah would remain in our home for three weeks. During that time, she would have a couple of overnight stays with the grandparents to help her adjust before moving there permanently. We would have her for the last weekend before she left in mid-November, 2009.

† † †

The next three weeks we tried to pack in all the love, hugs, kisses, prayers, and talks we could muster, given our fragile emotional state. One friend said, "I don't know how you will get through this, but I know you will."

Most days, we felt as if we were in a dream. We were eating and sleeping, loving Sarah, paying our bills, and visiting family with her for one last time. But we were also in shock, somewhat detached, always searching for the next best thing to say to Sarah or the next best thing to do with her. Intact biological families who live together forever don't face this split between the head and heart. They get to take for granted the luxury of eating Cheerios for breakfast and watching cartoons and saying supper prayers and reading bedtime stories without knowing it will be one of the last times to do those things together.

The impending doom weighed us down. We dipped into all the emotional and spiritual resources we had. Part of our saying good-bye involved seeing every moment as a last moment. We tried to convey through our words and actions that we didn't want to send her away, that we wanted her as our forever child. But there was a cosmic catch. Her being our forever child wouldn't mean she would live with us and grow up in our home and have a party given in her honor for high school graduation or be walked down the marriage aisle with Daddy Al. It would mean we would love her from afar and hold her in our hearts, wanting the best for her always and grieving the fact that we wouldn't be the ones with her every day.

All of that is hard to tell a young child, but we tried. In our first conversation with her, Al and I sat on the couch with her between us. Now was the time to begin.

"Al, you go first," I said. He groaned and took a deep breath.

"Sarah, how would you like to live in a new home?"

"Daddy, I already am home," she shot back.

Al and I looked at each other and he pointed to me. "OK, your turn."

"Sarah, did you know that in a couple of weeks you will not only visit your grandparents, but you will live with them all the time. What do you think about that?"

She stared at me and then at Al and asked, "Daddy, can we watch a movie?"

Recently, she had begun to focus more on books, media, and chocolate milk. We had a growing sense that these conversations could not be long. And in this case, she herself cut it short, though we could tell she had gotten the message. I secretly was glad she could not sustain more than a couple of minutes talking about *the* topic. I was emotionally spent, having put a foot in the waters that would only get deeper.

I learned to have these talks as we were doing an activity together. One evening after bath and books, we sat on her bed with a dry erase board as I told the story of how Sarah had two homes—ours and her grandparents. I drew two nearly identical houses, but ours with cats and theirs with a dog. I drew a walkway between them. I had hoped Sarah would make a connection between the two, something to the tune of how she visits both homes and that both families love her very much.

What she came up was deeper still and blew me away.

"Sarah, what is the same between these two homes even though they are different?" I asked. "Your grandparents have a dog, and we have a cat. They have a baby son and we don't have any other children." She gazed at my crude drawings, scrunched up her nose and jiggled her legs against the purple sheets. I asked again. "Sarah, what is the same about these two homes?"

"Sarah!" she said in pure innocence, telling me she was the one who belonged to both homes. She was the common factor.

My tears dripped onto the dry erase board, making a mess of my drawings. She had seen me cry so much in the last couple of weeks that my emotions were old hat to her. "Mommy, are you sad *again*?" She wiped away my tears with her little fingers. "Don't be sad, Mommy."

I pulled her next to me. "Oh, Sarah, I love you so much. Please remember that. In a couple of weeks, you will go and live with your grandma and grandpa in your new home. But just like you told me, honey, you will be the same person, no matter where you live. And you will be the one we will love forever."

As we went to bed, I felt grateful some of our attempts to explain this bizarre chain of events seemed to be sticking. But those little chats didn't always turn out the way I hoped. One morning about a week before she left, she and I were having breakfast at the kitchen table. She was eating Cheerios, and I was eating a scrambled egg.

Al and I had talked with a child therapist to help us learn how to best navigate these waters with Sarah. The therapist encouraged us to go as far in dialogue as possible and to be as clear as possible about what was coming. We had come to the point when we identified a day in November as the day she would leave. We circled that date on the calendar and marked off the days together. That was an important milestone to reach in our discussions, but the one that was outstanding was the toughest yet for me.

I took a deep breath and a few more swigs of coffee. I watched as she fidgeted with her cereal and hummed to "Bingo." She smashed a grape and flipped it with her spoon across the table to me.

"Sarah, we aren't giving you away." I looked at her sideways, praying for grace. Knowing that blaming courts and judges was something even her bright little mind couldn't understand, I nervously babbled on. "The *judge* has decided you are going to live with your grandparents. But *we* aren't giving you away."

"Oh, yes, you are," she shot back, boring into me with a look I'll never forget.

During the last weeks in our home, sometimes we struck out, like the "giving you away" discussion, and sometimes we hit it right. Al and Sarah came up with one of the deepest connections of all, one so characteristic of their trusting relationship. I tended to use too many words. Al simply let it happen on its own. I was constantly humbled to see they needed no help from me to reach the solid bottom line, a line that always shifted in my thinking.

One day when I was meeting with a client, I came home to Al, grinning from ear to ear. "You won't guess what Sarah came up with today." He beamed, the proud papa.

"What?" I asked.

"We were playing in the car, and she was in the back seat and I was in the front. I looked at her reflection in the rearview mirror and she launched into this thing about skin color.

"Daddy, Mommy's skin is white and my skin is white," she said. "But your skin is brown." With that pronouncement, she threw her arms around his neck and hugged him tight. "But that's OK. Daddy, because brown is my favorite color."

Al continued. "I said, 'But honey, I thought *purple* was your favorite color?'

"Well, it was, but now brown is. I love you, Daddy."

† † †

Gatherings with family and friends filled the last couple days. At my sister's house on the weekend before Sarah left, we threw a scrapbook party. I bought a scrapbook and colored paper and had copies made of photos I'd taken of Sarah and our family during the past months. On Friday evening I lugged these materials to Jane's where we spent the evening eating pizza and creating a scrapbook for Sarah to take with her. Each family—Jane and Vaughn and my two nieces and nephew and their families—created a page or two of their favorite photos of Sarah along with words of love.

On the Sunday night before she left on Tuesday, we had a book party and had Sarah's other significant people bring a favorite children's book. We asked them to write a message inside the book cover and then read it to Sarah during the party. One of my artsy-craftsy friends created a big pillow for Sarah, with different shades of purple cloth that Sarah helped choose, and a picture of the three of us appliquéd to the front on a big heart.

Our therapist had suggested that in addition to shaping images in Sarah's heart through talks, we also needed to provide tangible objects she could take with her. Though she would not be able to touch and feel us, she could touch and feel the smooth books and the soft pillow. They were not our hugs and kisses, but they could jar loose memories of those affections. Even though it didn't seem like much, it would have to be enough.

† † †

On the morning of the day Sarah was to leave at noon, my elderly father came over to make pancakes and sausage for breakfast. It was the meal our clan always thought of making during celebrative family gatherings. This time eating together around the table was small comfort in the midst of big pain.

Al and I looked at each other, and he nodded towards me, his cue that he would not be able to pray this morning. But neither could I, so I looked over at my father, the patriarch, and said, "Dad, would you pray?" And for the millionth time in my life, my dear father prayed to our Heavenly Father, a prayer *like* so many others, a prayer *unlike* so many others.

"Dear Heavenly Father, we come to you today so grateful for our family and for your love," he said, his gray head bowed, his face lined with all the journeys, dead-ends, and cul-de-sacs of life. "Today we ask that you let Sarah know how much we love her and how much she will always be part of our family." His voice quavered and he wiped his nose with his age-spotted hand. "Amen."

After we ate in somber quietness, I asked Sarah if she wanted to watch a movie with Grandpa. By this time, she had drawn into herself and did not smile or look directly at anyone. She got up from the table and went to the television by herself. I nodded to Dad to follow and he did. Dad sat on the couch next to Sarah and asked if she wanted to sit on his lap. Usually affectionate and trusting with him, she stayed about three feet away from him. Dad looked at me with sad eyes and I left their space, unable to deal with the forlorn separateness Sarah was trying to achieve.

A little later, she sat in the bay window, staring out of the glass and listlessly fingering her dolls and books. Al went to the window and stood behind her, wrapping his arms around her body and gazing out the window with her. They watched as a tree-wrecking crew across the street buzzed down a big tree which had grown diseased and old. I wrapped my arms around both of them. I remembered that the day we received the judge's verdict, it was one of the trees in our cul-de-sac that had thrashed wildly, mirroring my grief. This day, as we looked out, the tree in our neighbor's backyard was gone forever. But the stump remained, lined with indelible circles indicating that years of growth had indeed taken place on that very spot.

We stayed at that window until the grandparents drove into our driveway in their SUV. The grandparents and their little son came to our front door. There were trips out with Sarah's stuff, and we snapped pictures of Sarah with her biological family and Sarah with us, her bonded family.

We discussed visitation possibilities and agreed our first visit with Sarah would take place within a week from this day. As we finalized these plans, Sarah led the boy to the SUV. The grandpa strapped his son into the car seat as I helped the grandmother strap Sarah into hers.

My face close to hers, I said, "Oh Sarah, you know I'll love you forever, and Al and I are part of your forever family. We'll see you in a week." Usually so verbal, she stared at me without saying a word, her eyes filled with shock and confusion, her expression shut down. As I continued my good-bye, Al stood on the stoop. He had said his good-byes earlier, much more subtly. His good-bye had included the silent watching of the felled tree.

She continued to stare deep into me in a way that's all hers with wisdom beyond her years. My prayer was that somehow, in a pure child's way of knowing the truth, she believed we had dedicated ourselves wholly to carrying her across dangerous waters to the safety of the other shore.

The SUV circled out of our cul-de-sac and turned to go to Sarah's new home.

Al and I stood at the bay window, frozen in shock. As suddenly as she had dropped into our life, she was plucked from it. The SUV pulled out of sight. Al and I held each other, our arms aching for a group hug, for Sarah in-between. The empty space reminded us that love in families is not complete until shared. The circle of our love had been severed and the tattered ends of the broken circle hung limp and lost.

In the first months following Sarah's absence, I agonized most over what I imagined was her sense of abandonment, her sense of feeling she had been bad and that's why we gave her away. Nothing could be further from the truth. We had fought beyond all lost hope to embrace her as a beloved child who belonged with us.

I groped for an unreachable comfort in the day when working on my freelance stories, in the night when I lay in bed alone while Al was at work, in the midst of having coffee with friends, in my attempts at prayer. I needed something to sew up this gaping realization that I could never make this right for her. But I knew I was powerless to undo the damage. And it felt God was powerless too in the face of this suffering. I had spent years nurturing faith in a loving God. But in the blindness of my grief, I could not see God's hand at work creating a tapestry from these loose, ripped threads.

On more hopeful days, I realized no one could take away the experiences the three of us had shared. Between her entrance and exit in our lives, an eternity of mutual love had been forged, and a forever family had been born. It was a family that no one, no system, no law could destroy. It had been built on a foundation of emotional and spiritual bonding that transcended biology. For us, this bonding had become as strong as any blood tie, as binding as any kin.

SECTION FOUR

Reflecting on the Sarah Experience

Psalm 139:23–24 (NRSV)
Search me, O God, and know my heart;
test me and know my thoughts.
See if there be any wicked way in me,
and lead me in the way everlasting.

Note: The essays in this section examine our story from an academic perspective and provide some additional background for the concepts introduced in this book.

ESSAY ONE:

One-half Million and Doubling

When we began our process as foster parents, Al and I didn't have a clue about the scope of the foster and adoptive-care need that existed in America. Our love of children, our infertility, and our desire to be parents compelled our decisions. Though our desires were laced with altruistic compassion for children, alleviating stress for an over-burdened system was not on our radar.

When Sarah came to us in 2007, she was one of more than a half million American youth, from birth to eighteen, living in the foster care system, according to national statistics and state of Kansas numbers. More than 510,000 youth are in the system at one time.[1]

Since ASFA became law, the number of children in foster care on any given day has dropped somewhat. But timely adoptions still are not rising quickly enough to meet the increasing demand. Clues to why can be gleaned from a 2005 report released by The Evan B. Donaldson Adoption Institute, "Listening to Parents: Overcoming the Barriers to the Adoption of Children from Foster Care."[2] The report examines the reasons more than 90 percent of parent recruits do not end up adopting a child.

According to the report, each year nearly a quarter of a million Americans call social service agencies for information about adopting a child from foster care. But 78 percent who call for more information don't fill out an application or attend an orientation meeting. Only 6 percent of those who call for information actually complete the adoption home study, which is required for all prospective parents. Many people who complete a home study leave the child welfare agency without adopting.

The report shows that barriers that keep prospective parents from completing the process include differences between the types of child prospective parents seek, difficulties in accessing the agency, unpleasant initial contacts, and ongoing frustration with the process. Often, because of lag time in the system, children accrue a gathering roster of negative relational behaviors. This contributes to the fears potential families have about adopting a high-needs adolescent.

Conclusions of the report indicate that the most effective way to create permanent, loving homes for waiting children may not be to recruit more families. Rather, it may be to design the system to be more accessible and inviting for those willing and avidly trying to adopt a child from foster care.

ESSAY TWO:

Counting and Discounting Child Time

Bruce Perry writes of research regarding the effects of early childhood trauma in his book, *The Boy Who Was Raised as a Dog*, co-authored with Maia Szalavitz, an award-winning journalist.[3]

Perry's basic premise is: The younger a child, the more impressionable the brain, and the more deeply impacted the child is from stimulus absorbed environmentally. Perry explores on how the brain develops sequentially and most rapidly in the first years of life. That's why young children, whose brains are still developing, are at the greatest risk of suffering lasting trauma. The same plasticity that allows young brains to quickly learn love and language unfortunately also makes them highly susceptible to negative experiences. (p. 65)

"Just like a muscle, the more a brain system ... gets 'exercised,' the more it changes and the more risk there is of altered functioning," he writes. Exposing a person to chronic fear and stress is like "weakening the braking power of a car while adding a more powerful engine." (p. 66) Trauma alters the safety mechanisms that keep the car from going dangerously out of control.

Because of the impact of trauma on small children, guidelines are needed to help the courts make decisions in complicated cases rife with competing interests. One trustworthy guide is found in a landmark trilogy: *Beyond the Best Interests of the Child*, *Before the Best Interests of the Child*, and *In the Best Interests of the Child*, published between 1973 and 1986.[4]

The trilogy's authors, Joseph Goldstein, Albert J. Solnit, Sonja Goldstein, and Anna Freud, believe three important questions need to be asked: What set of principles should guide courts in their decision-making? What should justify state intrusion on the privacy of family relationships? And how should professionals—judges, lawyers, social workers, psychiatrists, and psychologists— pursue the *best interests* of children who have been abandoned, neglected, and/or abused?

The authors believe continuity of a child's relationship with his or her adult caregiver is universally essential to a child's well-being. Minimizing intrusions by the law is paramount to a child's healthy growth and development. Decisions must be based on preserving psychological parent-child relationships. In order to do this, professionals must be careful not to remove a child from their biological family too hastily. On the other hand, professionals should guard against reunifying children when it would allow the potential for further abuse and/or neglect. That could also mean honoring the trust-building experience by living long-term with a family who wants to adopt.

To keep children's needs paramount, the system must honor their needs for continuity of care and their sense of time. "The attachments of infants and toddlers are as upset by separations as they are promoted by the constant, unrationed, consistent presence, and attention of a familiar adult," the authors state. "When these children feel themselves abandoned by their parent, their distress leads to weakening their next attachments. Where continuity of such relationships is interrupted more than once, as happens with multiple foster placements in the early years, the child's emotional attachments become increasingly hollow and indiscriminate. They tend to grow up as persons who lack sustained warmth in their relationships." (p. 19)

The authors believe child placements should be as free of further state intervention and as permanent as the newborn relationship to biological parents, except for those in brief temporary care. Once prior ties have been substantially weakened, foster placements can no longer be considered temporary because it takes on the qualities of a psychological parent-child relationship, the authors state. And how is this relationship formed? Every child needs an unbroken relationship with at least one adult who alone, or together with others, is, and wants to be, directly involved and responsible for her daily needs. ... "Family ties need not depend upon the technicality of biological or legal relationships. When long-term foster parents return a child's affection and make her feel wanted, 'looked after,' appreciated, crucial attachments usually form, which ought not to be disturbed." (pp. 104-5)

The authors describe the damage that is done when this psychological parent-child relationship is not honored. "An erroneous wrenching of the nurturing bonds between the long-term foster child and his long-term foster family is the kind of damage that is not fully—or even substantially—recompensable even by ordering a resumption of the broken relationship," they write. (p. 108) This breaking of relationship is as unthinkable as would be an agency intentionally breaking a child's arm for some therapeutic purpose, believing that mistake will be corrected by resetting the limb.

Given this framework, these authors describe how the court must set in advance the maximum length of time for the placement. The authors suggest six months for a child up to the age of one month at the time of placement; twelve months for a child up to the age of three years at the time of placement; and twenty-four months for a child three years or older at the time of placement. These guidelines would account for the child's capacity in child time to sustain relationships with biological parents. (pp. 105-6)

"Emotionally and intellectually, an infant cannot stretch her waiting more than a few days without feeling overwhelmed by the absence of her parents," the authors state. "She cannot take care of herself physically, and her emotional and intellectual memory has not matured sufficiently to enable her to hold on mentally to the parent she has 'lost.' ... During such an absence, the child under two ... 'quickly' latches on to the new adult who cares for the child's needs. ... And for a child under five years, the absence of parents for more than two months is intolerable." (p. 41)

ESSAY THREE:

Best Interests:
Bonding or Blood?

The most frequent rationale for decisions regarding Sarah was: "They were made in the light of her best interests." We soon learned *best interests* was a multifaceted term, not one given to hard-core description or easily achieved. Though all of us wanted the best for Sarah, we were somewhat clouded by our agenda. The agency professionals needed to fulfill guidelines, timetables, and outcomes. The attorneys wanted to serve clients. The judge desired to rule fairly in a complicated situation. The maternal grandparents wanted justice for their biological family. Alfonso and I wanted to keep a child we deeply loved. And Sarah, because she was a vulnerable and dependent child, had no say in the matter. What would she have considered *best* if she had had a voice?

We often considered her best interests from our adult vantage point. No more helpful were legal definitions easily manipulated; they've been applied differently throughout the decades since the nineteenth century and the dawn of child welfare. Though there is no short definition for *best interests*, each U.S. state considers various factors in its deliberations. These are the state of Kansas guidelines:

- Consider the safety and welfare of a child to be paramount in all proceedings under the code;

- Provide that each child who comes within the provisions of the code shall receive the care, custody, guidance, control, and discipline that will best serve the child's welfare and the interests of the state, preferably in the child's home and recognizing that the child's relationship with such child's family is important to the child's well being;

- Make the ongoing physical, mental, and emotional needs of the child decisive considerations in proceedings under this code;

- Acknowledge that the time perception of a child differs from that of an adult and dispose of all proceedings under this code without unnecessary delay;

- Encourage the reporting of suspected child abuse and neglect;

- Investigate reports of suspected child abuse and neglect thoroughly and promptly;

- Provide for the protection of children who have been subject to physical, mental, sexual, or emotional abuse or neglect;

- Provide preventative and rehabilitative services, when appropriate, to abused and neglected children and their families so, if possible, the families can remain together without further threat to the children;

- Provide stability in the life of a child who must be removed from the home of a parent;

- Place children in permanent family settings, in the absence of compelling reasons to the contrary.[5]

These factors are substantial but can't clear up issues and questions. Should child welfare laws work for family preservation at all costs or strive for child protection at all costs?

Elizabeth Bartholet, Harvard Law School professor, describes this in her book, *Nobody's Children* [6]:

> "Family preservation has always been the dominant *modus operandi* in the child welfare system. The pendulum has swung back and forth, but always within a narrow scope. The choices for children have, accordingly, been defined narrowly. When the pendulum swings in the family preservation direction, we try to avoid removing children from their families at all costs and to return children who are removed as quickly as possible. When the pendulum swings in the opposite direction, we intervene more readily to protect children, removing them to foster or institutional care and leaving them there for long periods, formally tied to their parents, who retain parental rights and the opportunity to gain custody." (p. 24)

In her opinion, adoption, which includes severing the birth parents' rights and providing new parents for the child, should be a more viable option. Since the beginning of modern child welfare systems, adoption often has been reserved for exceptional situations. The custody battle in the final court hearing regarding Sarah's placement focused on a main theme: Should blood ties trump all other factors, including a deep bonding and attachment forged with a long-term foster family? Sarah's case was complicated by the fact that two sets of adoptive parents had been identified as suitable for her needs—one kin, the other not.

In the end, the judge ruled in favor of family preservation, returning her to extended biological family. Though she had lived with us for more than two years, the agency overturned its initial decision to choose us as the adoptive family, and the judge agreed. The rationale was that the strengths of the maternal grandparents had been underrated, and that in the end, Sarah's interests would be best served by returning her to kin. The long-term benefits of family reunification and identification with her kin would outweigh the short-term trauma of removal from our home.

Sarah's case, constellated around the competing forces of blood over bonding, is only one of hundreds of similar custody battles being waged in this nation's courtrooms. Federal and state laws have worked to incorporate more child-centered policies. But it is still very difficult for some professionals and parents to view children as individuals with needs rather than possessions. The work of the late Lloyd deMause and Alice Miller addresses this issue. deMause was director of The Institute for Psychohistory, editor of *The Journal of Psychohistory*, and president of The International Psychohistorical Association. Miller authored the best-selling *Drama of the Gifted Child*.

Lloyd's research shows that centuries of practices and attitudes have relegated children to the status of property to be manipulated and abused rather than persons to be nurtured. Modern laws have not successfully eradicated these premodern attitudes although the tide is shifting as parents, professionals, therapists, and child development specialists gain new skills and awareness.

"The history of childhood has been a nightmare from which we have only recently begun to awaken," said deMause during a lecture at the American Psychiatric Association Convention in Philadelphia. "The further back in history one goes—and the further away from the West one gets—the more massive the cruelty and neglect one finds and the more likely children are to have been killed, abandoned, beaten, terrorized, and sexually abused by their caretakers.

"Indeed, my conclusion from a lifetime of psychohistorical study of childhood and society is that the history of humanity is founded upon the abuse of children. ... Most historical families once practiced infanticide, erotic beating, and incest. Most states sacrificed and mutilated their children to relieve the guilt of adults. Even today, we continue to arrange the daily killing, maiming, molestation, and starvation of children through our social, military, and economic activities." [7]

Alice Miller in *Thou Shall Not Be Aware* [8] also examines the history of abuse. She believes adults are stilted in their ability to advocate for children. Because they are not healed from their own childhood traumas, openly facing the pain of their children is too threatening. So denial and thus maltreatment are recycled. Miller writes:

"For millennia it has been permissible and customary for children to be used to satisfy a wide variety of adult needs. They have provided a source of cheap labor, an ideal outlet for the discharge of stored-up affect, a receptacle for unwanted feelings, an object for the projection of conflicts and fears, compensation for feelings of inferiority, and an opportunity for exercising power and obtaining pleasure." (p. 310)

Her research demonstrates people today are still fully in favor of child-rearing practices used "for their own good"—beating, tormenting, demeaning, and humiliating.

The result of such denial is that many cases of maltreatment go unreported or underreported, but Bartholet's research indicates an estimated three million children suffer from serious forms of abuse and neglect each year. [9]

Hundreds of these children die. The National Child Abuse and Neglect Data System (NCANDS) reported an estimated 1,760 child fatalities in 2007. This translates to a rate of 2.35 children per 100,000 children in the general population. NCANDS defines "child fatality" as the death of a child caused by an injury resulting from abuse or neglect, or where abuse or neglect was a contributing factor. [10]

Despite the growing alarm in the increasing numbers and severity of abuse and neglect, the overloaded Child Protective Services system is not capable of treating all but the most severe of maltreatment cases, Bartholet writes. Increases in poverty and the decrease of available social services, coupled with increases in drug abuse, particularly crack and cocaine, are factors in these increases.

Also, state laws have defined abuse and neglect in ways designed to exclude all but the most serious forms of maltreatment. Legislators and judges have narrowed the definitions in reaction to earlier eras when many thought the categories were vague and inclusive. Statutes in the majority of states limit child abuse to acts that cause or threaten to cause lasting harm to the child.

Changes in the system are needed to promote adoption as a viable and healthy alternative, not as a last ditch resort, Bartholet asserts. Changes in the system could help meet growing demands for loving, psychological homes for children who are in abusive biological homes and for those who age out of the system and end up with no home at all.

"Child Protective Service (CPS) agencies are now devoting their resources to the many cases in which children remain in foster or institutional care for extended periods or bounce back and forth between foster homes and their original homes. We could reduce the burden on CPS by moving many more of these cases on to adoption at much earlier stages."

Bartholet knows it is difficult to find appropriate adoptive homes for children within the current system even if those children are currently freed up for adoption. "But this is because we have a system that holds children too long in their homes of origin and in out-of-home care until they have suffered the kind of damage that makes it hard for them to adjust and bond in a new family." [11] (p. 242)

ESSAY FOUR:

The Future of Foster-to-Adopt Parents

After Sarah was removed from our home, we revoked our foster-care license. We needed time to heal. But we also realized we were not the best candidates for the foster-to-adopt category. In retrospect, it may have been better for us to become licensed as a respite home. That's where children go for a day or a weekend to give foster families a break. Or, we could have chosen the foster category in which the child stays temporarily. The foster-to-adopt niche requires that the family walk a narrow tight rope between gain and loss, loving and letting go, certainty and limbo.

Ada Schmidt-Tieszen, professor of social work at Bethel College in North Newton, Kansas, describes the role of foster-to-adopt parents in her doctoral research, "Walking the Tightrope: The Role of Resource Parents in Concurrent Planning." Foster-to-adopt parents help the system work towards family reunification while, at the same time, developing an alternative permanent plan. This contrasts with traditional sequential case management in which reunification efforts are made and then, if unsuccessful, termination of parental rights and a search for another permanent home is begun.

Though concurrent planning helps the system to work toward its goals of family reunification and adoption, it can be a pressure cooker for foster parents, as Al and I discovered. She cites a focus group member in California who said foster-to-adopt parents felt schizophrenic in their role. They are asked to love the child like their own and be open to having a permanent role in the child's life. At the same time, they serve as a support and mentor for the birth parents to help them successfully reunify with the child.

Because the experience is a roller coaster ride, support is needed to help these families stay focused on the child's needs for permanency even as they normalize their own feelings of helplessness.

For her research, Schmidt-Tieszen conducted interviews with foster-to-adopt parents who shared suggestions for how the system could provide additional support for people willing to tackle this challenging role. The most distressed parents were those whose foster child was reunified with her family. Their need to grieve a loss that feels like a death, when no one has died, brings a lack of understanding and acknowledgement from their communities. They need social workers to be compassionate when others misunderstand.

Some people Schmidt-Tieszen interviewed described their loss as "worse than death." The pain arises from disenfranchised grief that cannot be publicly validated or openly mourned and results in intensified anger, guilt, and powerlessness. For some who had previously experienced grief with infertility or miscarriage, the loss of a concurrent planned child might have reopened old wounds. When earlier grief remains unresolved and is triggered anew, there can be "almost double the effect" of the loss.[12]

Schmidt-Tieszen's interviews with foster-to-adopt parents revealed many emotions. They included depression, denial and suppression of anger or sadness, reduced energy and ability to bond with a subsequently placed child, anger at the agency, and withdrawal from further work with the agency.

Some of the interviewees told Schmidt-Tieszen that child welfare agencies and social workers could assist the families with loss and grief in several ways:

- Allow time for grieving;
- Secure and fund grief counseling;
- Create and promote rituals for grieving;

- Better train parents for the challenges in this particular role;
- Help foster-to-adopt families discern, along with biological families, appropriate contact with the child after reunification.

Rituals promote expression of emotions, facilitate remembrance, and allow humans beings to acknowledge and accept change, Schmidt-Tieszen writes. The large number of resource parents in her study who used spirituality or religion as sustaining resources indicates religious sites or churches can be meaningful locations for these rituals.

In a secular vein, foster or adoption support groups might plan an annual ritual of remembrance and transition for those who have weathered the reunification of a child during the year, she writes. They could share stories and photographs and the solace of others who understand their pain and could also talk of the strengths and resilience garnered through adversity. Individualized decisions should be made about when and if resource parents will have contact with the birth family and the child who was removed from their home.

Schmidt-Tieszen's study explores how child welfare agencies consider that an ongoing relationship between the foster-to-adopt family and the reunified child is ideal. Open adoption includes frequent and ongoing presence or connection with all parenting parties in order to support the child.

In her study, some foster-to-adopt parents thought regular contact gave them an ongoing role to play, helped them gradually withdraw emotionally, and reassured them the child was well cared for. This contact facilitated grief, brought some closure with the loss, and offered evidence of their contribution to the life of the child and family. However, two foster-to-adopt families chose to discontinue contact because it was too painful.

In her Bethel College senior paper, Kayla Hiebert, one of Schmidt-Tieszen's social work students, also studied the foster-to-adopt experience. Hiebert interviewed Al and me for her 2010 study, "Forever Family: A Study of the Foster-to-Adopt Parent-Child Relationship, Coping Strategies, Motivations and Resources." [13] She asked what changes we'd like within the system. We said that a year-long after-care program would be ideal. Along with losing Sarah, we lost the support of social workers whom we had come to trust and share our lives with on a deep level. The adoptive family has the option of after-care for one year, but nothing is currently in place for foster-to-adopt families.

Having supports such as after-care and incorporating grieving rituals could have affirmed us and helped validate our experience. Walking alone through our sorrow, we were tempted to ask: Was our home just a hotel? Was our love simply damage control? Was our 24-7 care only glorified child care? But we knew without a doubt we had wholly dedicated ourselves to Sarah, and, yes, our hearts were broken when she left. Social workers cannot do everything. But they could agree to face the reality of inadequate procedures which finalized Sarah's move from our home. Al and I and most importantly, Sarah, will live forever with the pain and joy of our experience together.

Afterword
Fall 2010

After much prayer and discernment, shaped by counsel from family, church family, friends, and therapists, Al and I decided to continue regular visits with Sarah. We believed that the temporary confusion elicited by such visits would be worth the long-term benefits to Sarah, Al, and me.

Thankfully, the grandparents were gracious and complied with our wishes. The first visit occurred a week after she left and included a one-hour lunch of burgers and ice cream.

The next several visits occurred every two weeks and were three hours long. We generally took her to Applebee's, one of her favorite restaurants. We always sat in the same booth, and she always asked for a purple balloon. Sometimes we stopped at Wal-Mart to help her pick out clothes, shoes, or toys, or we went to the park. After a couple of months, we all settled on three-hour visits every three weeks. But the visits became less frequent.

Though these times are precious, they are not without heartbreak. During the first visit after we took Sarah home, her grandmother said, "Tell Al and Laurie good-bye."

Confusion spread across her face and she looked at me accusingly, "I thought *you* were my mommy?" I caressed her head and hugged her but was speechless with grief. There was no way for me to convey to her that we had not abandoned her. We were no longer the people she thought we were, and she likely felt betrayed. Though we had agreed with the grandparents we would work at being called Laurie and Al, it still felt unnatural. And to Sarah, the wise innocent one, it probably made no sense. You could not change names like you changed clothes, or paint over the images of our parenting on Sarah's life with a change in address.

Each parting had its anxiety, like the time she hung her head and sobbed and said, "I want to go home." We tried our best to show it was OK for her to feel her feelings, and we tried to synchronize with them. But in the end, she had to go inside and we had to drive away.

For some visits, it became her custom to say, "I want you back," after which we would say, "We want you back, too, Sarah. But now you are with your other family who loves you very much. But it is OK to feel sad and lonely. We do, too. We miss you and we will always come back to visit. We will always love you."

During these dialogues, we feel a responsibility to walk the emotional tightrope between openly grieving our loss and modeling for Sarah how to cope well. It's our hope and prayer that God will grant both families the grace to walk this tightrope with her, to hold her hand, to catch her when she falls. We need to help her make a good transition from our home to her new home. At the same time, we need to convey that we will not disappear nor abandon her.

† † †

The ability to provide this balance did not come easily to Al or me. We strove to heal some of our grief together and separately. In the first few months after she left, we did some joint counseling. Later on, we found some separate avenues. Some of my avenues included long bike rides, sharing with a spiritual director and prayer journaling. His avenues included writing letters to Sarah in the journal he kept during his prayer hour at church. Sister Mary Ellen Loch, CSJ, suggested he write letters that he could send to her later in her life. Here are three of those letters:

June 26, 2010
Dear Sarah,

It has been almost eight months since the judge said that you had to go live with your grandparents. I know it was hard for you to adjust to this move from our home. But I hope and pray you will be able to grow, with God's plan in your heart.

I earlier wanted to write to you about my feelings and thoughts, but I could never find the time. But starting today, I hope to keep in touch with you about my feelings, in hopes that one day you will read this and know that Laurie and I loved you with all our hearts and wanted the very best for you. I also wanted you to know that Laurie and I did not want you to leave our home – but the judge ordered it. Even though our hearts were broken by his decision, we wanted you to be happy with your new home and family.

As I sit in this Adoration Chapel on a Monday morning, thinking and praying about you, I know God has plans for you. This is the end of the first of many letters I plan to write to you.

God bless you, my forever daughter,
love your forever father, Dad

June 28, 2010
Dear Sarah,

Laurie and I just got back from her family reunion – the same one you attended the day after we first got you when you were five months old. I was happy and sad at the same time. Even now I am not sure what I should be feeling. More than ever, I want you back with us in our home. I miss your sweet voice and your many questions and demands. I miss the way you saw life and expressed yourself about it. By you leaving, I'll never really know what kind of relationship you and I would have had. But I know it would have been filled with a lot of love.

But even now when you are not with us, I still feel the love between us has become even stronger than ever. At times, I can still hear your voice and feel the warmth of your little girl hugs. I hope and pray you will never forget how much Laurie and I love you and will always be there for you.

To my forever daughter,
love always, your forever Dad

Aug. 28, 2010
Dear Sarah,

It has been almost a month since I last wrote you. I have been pretty busy with a full-time job, another part-time job and home life. Laurie and I have been busy taking care of the house and other family matters. We have also spent a lot of time praying about you, thinking about you and missing you – it seems like we miss you more each day. You are still too young to understand how much of "you" is still left in our home and in our hearts. Last Thursday, August 19, marks a month since we've last seen you. My heart pounded faster when I saw your eyes. My ears were straining to catch every sound that came out of your mouth. And holding you felt like I was holding all the gold in the world. I hope you still have feelings for Laurie and me. When I think about all that has happened to you in your three and a half years of life, I am thankful that God has poured out his grace and blessing on you. I am so glad God created you to be who you are! Sarah, you have many God-given gifts. Please don't let them go to waste. I pray that we will get to see you use those gifts and share them with others. Remember as you grow older that Laurie and I will always be there for you.

To my forever daughter.
love always, your forever Dad.

† † †

Just as we are striving to adjust, we hope and pray that Sarah is adjusting, too. But Sarah's feisty spirit, coupled with trauma-induced need for control, is keeping the transition from flowing easily, quickly, or smoothly. And our transition is grisly and bumpy, too. There is a part of us that doesn't want her to adjust completely. Because we are human and have parental needs for affirmation, we want her to miss us, to make sure she never forgets us. On the other hand, our task now as part of a large circle of forever family, is to become doting auntie and uncle figures. We need to remain in her corner, cheering her on, praying with her and for her, playing with her, reassuring her of our love. We need to help her to cope with the world the way it is, not the way we wish it would be or the way it was. That task requires we do the same. May we accept what we've been given and trust our good and loving God for the bigger plan. And within the grace of believing God is present, perhaps we will model for Sarah why sometimes it is a good thing to step into the raging rivers of life. We will model what it means to hold the hand of the One who created her and trust him to bring her across the iciest and swiftest of rivers. And now Sarah's Creator—along with her blood family—will nurture her into adulthood where she might carry others across the rapids to safe shores.

As I drove with Al to pick up Sarah for a recent visit, I pulled the car over to the side of the road to weep. "Honey, I don't know if I can do this. It's just so hard."

Unsure of what to do next, my husband said, "Do you want to go back home and cancel our visit? Is that what we need to do?"

I searched his face for some thread of strength, some thread of hope. "Sweetheart, remember how we committed to each other that either way— whether Sarah stayed or left—we would be her forever family?" he asked. "Well, now is the time to decide. Are we going to be that forever family or not?"

A sliver of clarity poked through my despondency. As always, he said more in a few words than most philosophers do in long speeches.

Making my choice, I started up the car and drove on toward Sarah. I did not know then, nor will I ever know what to expect. But one thing I do know for certain. Al and I won't continue our journey—be it in person or from afar—without forever carrying Sarah with us.

THE END

NOTES TO SECTION FOUR

[1]Adoption and Foster Care Analysis and Reporting System and the National Data Analysis System (Child Welfare League of America, 2006).

[2]Jeff Katz, "Listening to Parents: Overcoming the Barriers to the Adoption of Children from Foster Care." (New York: The Evan B. Donaldson Adoption Institute, 2005).

[3]Bruce Perry and Maia Szalavitz, *The Boy Who was Raised as a Dog*. (New York: Basic Books, 2006).

[4]Joseph Goldstein, Albert J. Solnit, Sonja Goldstein, and Anna Freud, *The Best Interests of the Child: The Least Detrimental Alternative* (New York: The Free Press, 1996).

[5]"Child Welfare: Determining the Best Interests of the Child," (Washington, DC: U.S. Department of Health and Human Services Administration for Children and Families, State Statute Results: Kansas, 2009). http://www.childwelfare.gov/systemwide/laws_policies/state/index.cfm?event=stateStatutes.processSearch.

[6]Elizabeth Bartholet, *Nobody's Children: Abuse and Neglect, Foster Drift and the Adoptive Alternative* (Boston: Beacon Press, 1999).

[7]Lloyd deMause, "The History of Child Abuse," (speech presented to American Psychiatric Association, Philadelphia, Pa., 1994).

[8]Alice Miller, *Thou Shalt Not Be Aware: Society's Betrayal of the Child.* (New York: Farrar, Strauss and Giroux, 1987).

[9]Bartholet, *Nobody's Children.*

[10]The National Child Abuse and Neglect Data System (NCANDS). U.S. Department of Health and Human Services, Administration on Children, Youth and Families, 2007.

[11]Bartholet, *Nobody's Children*.

[12]Ada Schmidt-Tieszen, "Walking a Tightrope: The Role of Resource Parents in Concurrent Planning." (Ph.D. diss., University of Kansas, 2004).

[13]Kayla Hiebert, "Forever Family: A Study of the Foster-to-Adopt Parent-Child Relationship, Coping Strategies, Motivations and Resources." (Bethel College, North Newton, Kan., 2010).

BIBLIOGRAPHY

Awdry, The Rev. W. *Thomas the Tank Engine.* London: Edmund Ward & Co., 1946.

Bartholet, Elizabeth. *Nobody's Children: Abuse and Neglect, Foster Drift and the Adoptive Alternative.* Boston: Beacon Press, 1999.

Brown, Margaret Wise. *Goodnight Moon.* New York: Harper, 1947.

Carle, Eric. *The Very Hungry Caterpillar.* New York: Philomel Books, 1987.

Cline, Foster W. and Jim Fay. *Parenting with Love and Logic: Teaching Children Responsibility.* Colorado Springs: Pinon Press, 2006.

deMause, Lloyd, ed. *The History of Childhood.* New York: Harper & Row, 1974.

Disney Enterprises, Inc. / Pixar Animation Studios, *Finding Nemo?* Oakland, Calif.: 2003

Flaming, Maria. *Where Do Kisses Come From?* New York: A Golden Book, 1999.

Goldstein, Joseph, Albert J. Solnit, Sonja Goldstein, and Anna Freud. *The Best Interests of the Child: The Least Detrimental Alternative.* New York: The Free Press, 1996.

Hill, Eric. *Where's Spot?* New York: G.P. Putnam's Sons, 1980.

Miller, Alice. *Drama of the Gifted Child.* New York: Basic Books, 1996.

Miller, Alice. *Thou Shalt Not Be Aware: Society's Betrayal of the Child.* New York: Farrar, Strauss and Giroux, 1987.

Milne, A. A. *Winnie-the-Pooh.* New York: Dutton's Children's Books, 2005.

Munsch, Robert. *I'll Love You Forever*. Willowdale, Ont.: Firefly Books Ltd., 1986.

Perry, Bruce, and Maia Szalavitz. *The Boy Who was Raised as a Dog*. New York: Basic Books, 2006.

Taylor, James. *James Taylor's Greatest Hits*. U.S.A: Warner Bros. Records Inc., 1976.

Vischer, Phil, *Bob and Larry's ABC's, Veggietale Series*. Franklin, Tenn.: Big Ideas, Inc., 1997.

ACKNOWLEDGEMENTS

This book was made possible through the undying love, support, and prayers of my husband, Al, and my family of origin – namely my sister, Jane Lambert, my father, Paul Oswald, and both our extended families. The care of family during the sojourn with Sarah and the writing project became "Christ with skin on" for me.

This book was also made possible by the many gifted professionals and readers who helped birth it. Professor Ada Schmidt-Tieszen infused my project with a balance of academic rootedness and warm heartedness. Judy Entz, Mennonite Press, was a joyful and prayerful supporter and provided a bridge to the print shop professionals, namely Jim L. Friesen, who helped bring this book home. I especially appreciated copy editor June Galle Krehbiel and proofreaders Serese Mattek and Denise Rhoades. Many readers helped to sharpen the book as it morphed through many drafts: Joanna Bjerum, Michael Combs, Carol Duerksen, Heather Fischer, Michele Hershberger, Kayla Hiebert, Jane Lambert, Katherine Mick, Emily Nash, Paul Schrag, Wendy Schrag, Linda Shelly, Kris Timmermeyer-Rice and Bev Wiebe.

Friends provided moral support when I became unsure about whether this book should proceed. Susan Morton encouraged me to reach beyond my fears to faith. Many other friends believed in me along the journey: Pastor Joan Boyer, Lori Kennell, Sue Illiano, Daneille Schmidt, the Life Sharing Sunday school class at First Mennonite Church in Newton, Kan., and fellow members at Our Lady of Guadalupe, Newton.

Elaine Maust, spiritual director, and Victoria Darkey walked me through grief and absorbed my tears during the writing. Other spiritual directors who provided comfort and clarity were Gene and Mary Herr and Sister Mary Ellen Loch, CSJ. The Sisters of St. Joseph in Wichita, Kan., Carol Duerksen and Maynard Knepp, Bev and Chuck Regier and Mike and Marlene Bogard provided cloistered spaces for writing marathons.

Though it was difficult to be grateful for them at the time, I now thank the professionals and social workers who engaged with us during the past three years. I now see you cared deeply for Sarah, even though systemic complications sometimes clouded that caring.

Last of all, I thank the Lord Jesus Christ and Mother Mary for holding me together when the winds of grief tempted to scatter my broken mother's heart into a black hole of oblivion. Their presence brought me hope that suffering for the sake of forever family need never be in vain.

Laurie Oswald Robinson
Newton, Kansas
Sept. 28, 2010